PIVOTING DURING THE PANDEMIC

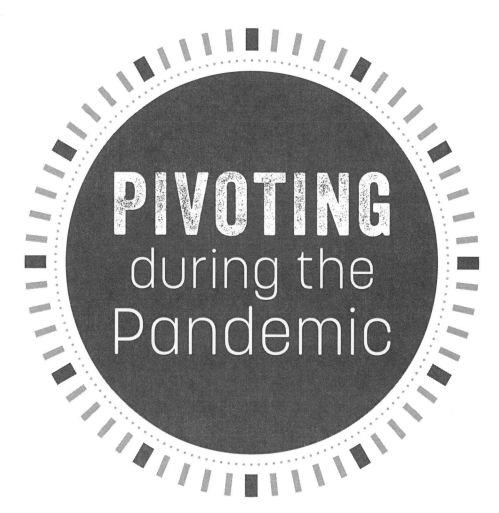

PIVOTING
during the
Pandemic

Ideas for Serving Your Community Anytime, Anywhere

edited by *Kathleen M. Hughes* and *Jamie Santoro*

ALA
Editions

CHICAGO | 2021

KATHLEEN M. HUGHES

is the editor of *Public Libraries* magazine and the manager of publications, Public Library Association.

JAMIE SANTORO

is a senior acquisitions editor with ALA Editions | Neal-Schuman.

© 2021 American Library Association

Extensive effort has gone into ensuring the reliability of the information in this book; however, the publisher makes no warranty, express or implied, with respect to the material contained herein.

Note: All Bitly links are case-sensitive.

ISBNs
978-0-8389-4974-0 (paper)
978-0-8389-4989-4 (PDF)

Library of Congress Control Number: 2020047213

Book design by Alejandra Diaz in the Kandal and Korolev typefaces.

♾ This paper meets the requirements of ANSI/NISO Z39.48-1992 (Permanence of Paper).

Printed in the United States of America
25 24 23 22 21   5 4 3 2 1

CONTENTS

Introduction ix
The Anytime, Anywhere Library

Contents

Contents

INTRODUCTION

The Anytime, Anywhere Library

I n March 2020 American public libraries (along with the rest of the world) began experiencing the fallout from the COVID-19 pandemic. Buildings were closed, services interrupted, programs suspended. With no library pandemic playbook and no clear epidemic management plan or communication from the federal government, public libraries were left scrambling to patch together safe and effective plans to continue providing services to their communities.

What did communities need? What was safe to do? How could library programs and services continue? Learning through trial and error, most libraries, though initially closed, soon sprang back into action and began to offer some socially distant in-person services like curbside pickup and outdoor storywalks. Other libraries expanded their virtual offerings to serve job-seekers, book lovers, older adults, and students. Still others addressed their community's increasing digital demands by providing tech support and hotspot devices to patrons.

In this collection of twenty-two reflections by library staff across the country, you'll read how public libraries responded to the challenges imposed by COVID-19 with their typical gusto, pivoting quickly to continue to provide exemplary services to their communities. You'll find ideas and tools to use as we ride out the current pandemic or face a similar event in the future. And if all goes as we hope, you'll finish the book feeling inspired, knowing that though COVID-19 has closed many real doors, many new "doors" have opened.

Does your library have a story to share about services that it developed or strengthened in response to COVID-19? Tell us about it.

— **KATHLEEN M. HUGHES**
khughes@ala.org

— **JAMIE SANTORO**
jsantoro@ala.org

FOSTERING SOCIAL CONNECTIONS AND LOCAL COMMUNITY DURING A GLOBAL PANDEMIC

— Shaun Briley —

L ibraries have long been adapting to competition from the internet in the form of affordable books delivered overnight by Amazon, a growing e-book market, and the ability to obtain the answers to many informational questions at the tap of a finger. Often we have reacted the same way that the retail sector has, by learning how to provide a user "experience" at our locations in order to supplement the "product." The focus of many libraries has been evolving away from collections and moving toward a role as the "third place," a physical community hub with increasing importance given to programs, events, and activities. There is political support for this, in part because libraries are acting as a kind of social cement that holds communities together.

Enter the COVID-19 pandemic.

Now, with our doors closed and gatherings not permitted, how do we provide that social connection and contribute to a sense of community? How do we advocate for ourselves during closures and budget cuts when our programs are such a large driver of our political support? In the face of Zoom fatigue and with so much quality content freely available online, what can the library provide that adds real value in this area?

Early indications suggest that people still want libraries to fill a social role during the pandemic, but don't necessarily have confidence that we can do so. In April the Mid-Continent Public Library system in Missouri started a substantial user survey to determine what patrons considered their biggest need during the pandemic. The largest response by far was "social interaction." At the same time, the survey identified the challenges libraries face in pivoting to an online platform, given the fact that 97 percent of typical library users said they had never attended virtual library programs, and only a little more than 20 percent indicated they were likely to do so. The findings were reported at the ALA Virtual Conference 2020 by Mid-Continent's library director, Steve Potter.

CITIZEN SCIENCE PROGRAMS FOSTER COMMUNITY

As libraries turn to the seemingly paradoxical concept of programs that people do on their own but also together, one of the most exciting options is citizen science. This is where individuals or families safely do a science-based activity on their own outside of the library and the library acts as the organizer, the disseminator, and the collector of results. There are many types of projects with important real-world objectives that involve getting outdoors to examine the flora and fauna in one's backyard or local park. Alternatively, some projects, like Eyes on Alz, involve sitting at a computer to help scientists trawl through brain scans looking for a cure for Alzheimer's disease. From the aspect of fostering community, the best projects are ones that look at a local issue; for instance, measuring air quality or light pollution at night. Organizations such as SciStarter, based out of Arizona State University, list many citizen science projects and detail how to get involved in them. It is even possible to "shop" the projects for their local relevance on the website (scistarter.org).

In San Diego before the pandemic, I was part of a project where a thousand kits were checked out by library patrons to collect insects and create an insect map for the city. This gave scientists an environmental baseline for the local food chain and insect pollinators, which in turn assists with understanding the impact of climate change. In Coronado, a beach community near San Diego, we sent teens out armed with their cell phones to take part in a survey of the state of our coastline. Now we are exploring participation with the Border Solutions Alliance in a COVID-19 data challenge.

There are often local museums or schools available to partner with. The role of the library in these projects is to be the community connector, bringing everyone together and especially bringing the "citizen" to citizen science. These types of projects reverse the usual paradigm, where folks go to the library to get a piece of information; instead, libraries crowd-source going out and creating new information by library patrons and the library community. The projects show the value and relevance of libraries by demonstrating our power to "bring the community together" to stakeholders in government and higher education, and they can also bring needed visibility to the library.

NEWSFLASH: LIBRARIES HAVE THE LOCAL SCOOP

Across the nation, local newspapers have been in long-term decline, a trend that has been accelerated by the pandemic. There may now be a greater need for some forms of nonpolitical local information, local connectivity of a newsy or entertaining nature, and a place for libraries to fill some of these gaps within our information remit. Prompted by the pandemic, our library here in Coronado has been producing a series called "Library Reports: Community Heroes" in which a librarian interviews local firemen, hospital workers, teachers, animal shelter staff, and so on. We invite them to talk about how the pandemic is affecting our community through their eyes. The short interviews are shown on Facebook, are available on YouTube, and are broadcast on our local Channel 19. The videos have provided excellent opportunities for cross-promotion and have generated the most views of anything our library has done during the closure, once again putting us in the role of a community connector. Through this project, there has actually been a strengthening of community relationships thanks to our collaboration with other local organizations that have taken part, and of course they have put the library in front of their own social media followers.

Now we are developing a new video series called "Library Reports: Local History." Serving as a vehicle for local history information is another area where the library can compete against the broader allure of the Web and foster a comforting sense of community nostalgia. For example, a topical segment could cover what happened in your community during the Spanish flu pandemic in 1918. All it takes is a bit of reference work, a smartphone, and a tripod. Some libraries have been preparing time capsules or collecting experiences connected with the pandemic for future generations. We have also worked on some public information videos; for instance, one on composting at home, and another about the responsible collection of sand dollars from the beach that was widely shared in the community.

TOGETHER AT HOME

When libraries first started participating in social media, some of us just posted a JPEG of our standard fliers—the old format of spreading information—which of course didn't take advantage of the possibilities of the new media. We have already come a long way in adapting and realizing that different media require different approaches. Likewise, we are learning during the pandemic that it is often not a successful approach to just take the old program and stick it online. Programs that translate well to an online format because they already involved doing something "together" but can be done at home include a "community read" and the just completed summer reading program. This year, we purposely opted out of our usual participation in iREAD in favor of a locally focused, environment-themed summer reading program in partnership with a nonpartisan environmental group based in town. The Coronado Public Library has had great success with crafts programs where patrons check out supplies via curbside pickup and then do something together via Zoom. Recently we checked out spices for a cooking challenge. We have been a partner in a local Neighbor-to-Neighbor phone tree that checks up on elderly and vulnerable residents to make sure nobody is stranded at home. This has generated a fresh pool of library volunteers for us.

One area where we have tried to mimic our former operations is by trying to provide a virtual meeting space for some of the groups that came and used our community hall before the pandemic. For instance, we have been using our commercial Zoom account to host open readings held by the San Diego Shakespeare Society. These meetings run over the time allotted by a free Zoom account. The commitment is pretty minimal on our part and basically consists of generating the event invitation to send to people who have registered for the event, greeting folks, the handover to the host, and monitoring the event for technical issues. In return, we are keeping the library's name out there and staying connected to people and groups that might not check out books ordinarily, but who look to us in our role as a community hub.

IT'S ABOUT YOU

The library's strongest asset in fostering social connections is of course its staff. There is still a lot of mileage in those quirky Facebook posts of staff members holding up their favorite book or demonstrating various ways to maintain social distancing. Postings that do well include familiar faces in front of familiar backdrops. Elsewhere in this book, our colleagues will discuss going online with regard to storytimes, book clubs, and interesting ways to offer personal reader's advisory while closed. It has been observed that the pandemic is accelerating societal trends such as the rise of teleconferencing and the decline of main street retail. Maybe for libraries the pandemic will encourage us to look out more, to be stronger and cleverer online about how we engage with our local communities. Here in California, the land of wildfires, we are very familiar with the concept of new seeds growing from the ashes.

ENGAGING YOUR COMMUNITY WITH DIGITAL AUTHOR EVENTS

— Stesha Brandon —

The pandemic has interrupted many of the usual ways that we engage patrons. As our libraries work to provide essential services and materials, digital programming can offer continuity of care. Virtual author programs remind patrons that they are not alone during this challenging time. Digital events are a way to be in our community together, even when we are separated physically.

But before you jump into the digital event space, there are some very basic questions to consider. What type of program is best for your patrons? Does an event with registration make sense? Or should you livestream your program on social media? What makes your program unique? How do racial equity and accessibility factor into your program plans?

As the Seattle Public Library has begun to offer digital author events, we have grappled with these questions and learned some lessons along the way.

LESSON 1 | BE PATIENT

Everything takes a bit longer than you'd expect. We're all learning new processes and routines, and in many cases, the infrastructure for virtual programs may still be being developed. Try to allow plenty of time in which to develop and implement each virtual program. Allow time for behind-the-scenes tasks like building registration pages, familiarizing yourself with your chosen digital platform, scheduling a practice session with your staff and speaker, and marketing the event to the public.

Try this: Aim to do a certain number of virtual programs each month, based on your staff capacity and budget constraints. Once you have that number of programs scheduled, stick to it. Make a timeline and checklist for all of the tasks that are required for each event. You will get more efficient at the checklist as you do more programming.

LESSON 2 | BE FLEXIBLE

This is an unusual time, and you may not be able to do the type of programs you're used to. You and your staff may need to learn new skills that are specific to virtual events. As much as possible, try to roll with the changes, be kind to yourself and others, and use this as an opportunity to learn.

Try this: Think local. Many of your local or regional authors may have had books released during the pandemic, and might appreciate the opportunity to do events to talk about them. Or consider running a writing class that features a local author as the instructor. Make a list of local writers, and identify any themes or possible pairings of authors for a program. But don't forget to "think big" as well. Because these programs are virtual, you may have the opportunity to host someone who wouldn't normally travel to your area. This is a great time to explore which nationally touring authors might be willing to do a digital program. Lots of publishers have library marketing departments that may be able to help you plan events. Consider pairing a nationally touring author with a local author in order to bring local context to your event and make it unique.

Example: The nationally touring author Cathy Park Hong discusses her recent book *Minor Feelings* with local professor Vince Schleitwiler: www.youtube.com/watch?v=lioInyQoKK4.

LESSON 3 | USE A GROWTH MINDSET

In many cases, the digital events will be a new venue for your programming. Consequently, there may be hiccups or things may go wrong. This is completely normal. Any time we're learning new skills and pivoting to deliver services in a different way, there are bumps along the road.

Try this: In advance of your event, think strategically. How will your event be set up? What problems might arise during the event, and how will you troubleshoot them?

Once you have your plan in place, you've done everything that you can do. After the event, assess what went smoothly and what could be improved. Try to integrate what you've learned into the next event that you're planning.

LESSON 4 | PARTNER UP

Many of the organizations that we would normally partner with have been deeply impacted by the pandemic. This time is a wonderful opportunity to partner with the community stakeholders that could use your support. Independent bookstores and small arts organizations have been particularly hard hit, and will make natural partners for your virtual author programs. And there are bonuses to working together: each organization can help amplify the event, and you'll also feel less alone as you work on the program together.

Try this: As you're planning each digital program, identify at least one community organization you can invite to partner on the event. Invite an independent bookstore to be the official bookseller for the program. Don't have a local independent bookstore in your town? Because book sales are online, your partner bookstore doesn't need to be in your town, and can still help to provide reach.

Or you can find a community partner with whom you have a relationship and invite them to develop a program with you.

Example: The Seattle Public Library's "Seattle Writes" program partners with a local writing center, Hugo House, to offer digital writing classes: https://bit.ly/32QLGS5.

LESSON 5 | COMMUNICATION IS KEY

As we work remotely and produce events digitally, our staff are more dispersed than they might usually be. This means it is particularly important to communicate with them about your virtual programs as early and as much as possible. Staff and patrons may have questions about a program and will need to know who to contact.

Try this: Create a place where all program details are collected, including the contact information for the program lead and contact. This will make it easy for front-line staff to answer patrons' questions about the programs, and direct any inquiries they can't handle to the program lead.

LESSON 6 | ASSESSMENT AND REFLECTION

How will you know if your virtual program was a success? What benchmarks will you use? Tracking the number of unique attendees is one metric that can

Planning Your Digital Program

Consider these questions when planning your digital program:

Budget

- Will your budget allow for a digital platform license?
- Will your budget allow you to pay speakers or instructors a modest honorarium?
- Is your budget supporting racial equity and accessibility?

Platform

- Which digital platform are you using? Is your program a webinar (presentation style) or a meeting (interactive style)?
- Are you streaming the program to social media?
- Practice using the platform, and familiarize yourself with the settings.

Registration

- Does your event require pre-registration? This can be the best way to ensure security for the event, but it may present a barrier to access for some.

Accessibility

- Is your event accessible to those with sensory impairments? Should you provide captioning or ASL interpretation?

Contingency Planning

- What could go wrong? (Your internet access goes down, the computer goes down, etc.)
- How will you respond if this happens? What can you do in advance to mitigate any potential issues?

Staffing/Hosting

- Who will be hosting the program? Who will manage the Q&A?
- Who will manage the tech side (the platform/streaming)?

Tech Check

- Set up a practice session with the speaker and staff who will be working. You can troubleshoot any potential issues in advance of the event. If your speaker isn't available for a tech check in advance of the event, set up a practice session with the staff and then invite the speaker to log on a bit early for the digital program in order to go over any questions they may have.

Marketing

- How will patrons find out about your virtual program?
- Have you invited your community partners to help spread the word?

Assessment and Reflection

- What metrics and benchmarks will indicate a successful program?
- How will you gather patron feedback?
- What did you learn from doing this program, and how can you use that information to improve your next program?

shed light on success, but you may also want to track the number of program views or engagement on your library's social media or YouTube channel. There are also qualitative ways to assess success, such as how engaged attendees are during the program. This can be estimated based on their use of the chat, Q&A, or comment functions. Many platforms allow users to send post-event surveys as well, and this can be an excellent way to check in with patrons about their program experience.

Finally, after the program, take some time to consider what worked and what could be improved for both the staff and the patron experience.

Try this: Before your program, determine what metrics you will gather and what benchmarks will indicate your program was a success. This can be as simple as a target attendance number, or it can be related to gathering patrons' comments or engagements. Set aside time the day after the program to consider how it went and to write down any reflections to be implemented as part of your next event.

STILL LEARNING

As the Seattle Public Library has pivoted to digital programs, we've learned many of these lessons firsthand. And we're still learning. We continue to grapple with how best to engage patrons who are not already in our digital space. That said, our community has responded positively to moving these events online. We've actually seen increases in attendance for author programs, and increased interest in the recordings we make available after the event. Many patrons have also taken the time to e-mail us to let us know how grateful they are for the programs. Books are a wonderful way for readers to connect with the world around us. During this pandemic, it seems more important than ever to read.

PROVIDING A SEAMLESS
VIRTUAL REFERENCE EXPERIENCE

— Lauren Seegmiller —

n March 2020, the world turned upside down, and library service was no exception. As the coronavirus, closures, and curbside service took root, many libraries pushed their online offerings to the forefront as library workers learned new ways to combine safety with service.

I arrived at librarianship well into the digital era. I even completed a fully online MLIS. Canvas was my classroom, and Slack and Zoom were my learning commons. I streamed commencement in my pajamas from 1,300 miles away. This experience could be profoundly isolating, but it also personally prepared me for closure (as much as anything could).

I have worked at the Denver Public Library (DPL) since 2013, and have been a librarian in the Reference Services Department there since 2017. Reference Services supports the wider library system as a sort of multi-format information desk/switchboard. Instead of one call center, all library branches have their own phone. Those calling the Central Library's main line often speak to Reference Services first. Our department also monitors the DPL's main e-mail queue and staffs the chat service. Reference uses Springshare's LibAnswers as our e-mail and chat platform, and participates in an international chat cooperative. Reference also supports many DPL appointment services by providing one-on-ones for students, entrepreneurs, patent-searchers, and grant-seekers (including online appointments when possible).

My situation is unusual. Our large, urban public library is blessed with a big staff and a strong IT infrastructure. So I've kept that in mind, and focused in this chapter on advice that can apply to a wide variety of library experiences.

EMBRACE VIRTUAL REFERENCE SERVICE

To paraphrase the Reference & User Services Association's 2017 guidelines: a virtual reference transaction is done remotely through some technological medium, such as e-mail, instant messaging (hereafter called "chat"), texting, VoIP, or videoconferencing.[1]

Society sprinted to close once the COVID-19 pandemic hit, but the consumer trend of staying at home has proved to be a marathon. Streaming, online shopping, social media, and delivery subscriptions had already changed our lives and our economy, and the pandemic has only accelerated these trends. By now, the option to chat with customer service is common among private companies. Before the DPL closed, some customers inside the building would ask questions via chat rather than approach the nearest staff desk. Ward and Barbier wrote that "chat is here to stay" in 2010, and they're still right.[2]

The DPL went from cautious cancellations to indefinite closure in about seventy-two hours. The robustness of our library's long-standing virtual reference service allowed Reference Services to keep seamless contact with customers even when the buildings and phones shut down. As non-Reference staff hurriedly developed VoIP procedures and virtual programming, we held the front line. Armed with VPN-enabled laptops from our IT department, we fielded a record number of chat questions on our first closed day—a record we would break more than once while closed.

Our library's heavy investments in virtual reference before the pandemic struck (and forced our closure) allowed us to expand and adjust our existing online services rather than build entirely new ones. Piloting business appointments with screen-sharing software in 2018 laid the track for moving our other appointment services online. We also executed a planned change in our chat platform in May 2020, while working from home. Our experience with virtual reference service at large helped us focus on mastering new details.

If you already do virtual reference, do you promote it? Our statistics show that chat at our library grew 45 percent between March and August of 2020. This was a big jump, but it's part of a years-long upward trend we've cultivated by increasing the number of embedded chat widgets and demonstrating chat service during school outreach. To market your virtual reference services, put a banner on your website, write a public blog post, demonstrate during a virtual program, and post fliers or print bookmarks. If you build it, they might come, but you should also consider advertising.

BUILD ON THE BASICS

It can be difficult to do a textbook reference interview online or asynchronously. Body language and tone cannot guide you, not everyone types fluidly, and it's awkward to type out something that could be demonstrated visually in seconds. However, the core of the reference interview still applies.[3]

It's tempting to skimp on the time spent on reference interviews online.[4] Chat feels urgent, and customer impatience or juggling multiple chat sessions can exacerbate that feeling. I find that taking the time to ask clarifying questions both fulfills my duty to the reference interview and stalls for time as I throw search terms into a database, seek a colleague's help, or answer another customer. It's okay to remind people that research takes time, and that you may have to follow up in order to give their question proper attention.

Asynchronous modes have a stop-and-start nature that can lose the reference interview. For example, DPL customers initiate our appointment services through online forms. Some submit single-word questions on the form, while others ask more questions than we could ever cover in one hour. I've found that failing to check in with them somehow (by summarizing their form answers, by asking them to tell me about their business, etc.) often means I've wasted time preparing to answer the wrong question. Good research takes time, and bad research takes extra time.

To serve customers over both chat and one-on-one videoconferencing, I try to explain to them everything I'm doing during the interview, all the time. These explanations fill empty space and also cultivate the teach-a-person-to-fish paradigm I strive for. By using screen-sharing, it's easier to narrate my navigation to the customer. In chat, I have to imagine I'm doing a video demonstration, and the text of the chat is my narration.

Try to find time-saving methods that won't shortchange customers. If you find yourself re-answering the same questions from different users, save the best versions of your answers as scripts, canned messages, or templates in order to save time. Some chat and e-mail services support these functions, but you can DIY them by creating drafts and docs to copy and paste.

Increasing from one to two staff per chat shift has helped us to manage the higher traffic during the pandemic. If you have a small staff, investigate joining a chat cooperative in order to offset the high volumes.

SHARING IS CARING (MOSTLY)

My most valuable research resource is my colleagues' experience. My preferred method of gathering their input used to be shouting over my cubicle wall for help. We created a departmental chat as a digital all-hands-on-deck resource for high-volume chat times. During work from home, that chat became our virtual workroom. It's our channel to ask for on-the-fly help, update colleagues, and drop morale-boosting cat photos. We use Google Hangouts, but Microsoft Teams or Slack also allow real-time conversation without creating e-mail clutter.

Asynchronous information-sharing is also important. As a big library system, the DPL has thrived on Google Drive for ages. Live updates to documentation are invaluable, and we have created a number of one-stop-shop documents to help our staff navigate a deluge of fast-coming changes to internal procedures and external resources alike.

Be clear on restrictions and regulations around customer privacy, work products, and open records laws. Libraries are ethically (and sometimes legally) bound to protect customers' privacy, a position sometimes contrary to the online environment.

BE A KNOW-IT-ALL (ABOUT YOUR LIBRARY)

My work motto is "Reference Needs to Know." If the public can ask about something, they will. Where is the bookmobile? How fast is your public Wi-Fi? Can we rent your library for our wedding? These days, there's even more to ask about because many library procedures have completely changed (and may change again during the reopening phases).

Decision-makers: Your greatest gift to front-line staff is information. Keep front-liners in the loop, be clear, prepare public talking points, and be available for questions and comments from them. Explain the reasoning behind any new processes and procedures, because customers will express frustration at any changes they encounter. I prefer to have too much information so that I can distill it for customers. Communicate widely: I prefer a redundant e-mail pointing me to a staff intraweb post, rather than missing new information.

Front-liners: The need to proactively address customers' needs has not changed. Take the customer's-eye view of changes, find potential pain points, and know who to ask about them. If your organization is prone to communication silos, ask decision-makers to include your department in updates, especially if you act as the first point of customer contact.

Institutional knowledge is necessary to establish boundaries and to provide consistent customer service. Know your public policies inside-out and navigate customers to them (ideally on your website). Established internal procedures will help defuse potentially difficult situations with customers.

TURN AND FACE THE STRANGE

Libraries have adapted to many social changes, but COVID-19 has mandated quick adaptation to the unknown. We have no idea what the future holds for public spaces. Expanding our virtual reference offerings is a way to provide a core library service in a socially distant format. And there's still room for exciting new possibilities. For example, the DPL's Western History and Genealogy Department recently purchased an overhead document camera to explore the possibility of giving researchers online access to archival collections. Witnessing library ingenuity in action is a beacon in a time shrouded in anxiety and uncertainty.

NOTES

1. Reference & User Services Association, "Guidelines for Implementing and Maintaining Virtual Reference Services," www.ala.org/rusa/resources/guidelines/virtrefguidelines.
2. Joyce Ward and Patricia Barbier, "Best Practices in Chat Reference Used by Florida's Ask a Librarian Virtual Reference Librarians," *Reference Librarian* 51, no. 1 (January 2010): 67, doi: 10.1080/02763870903361854.
3. Barry Trott and Howard Schwartz, "The Application of RUSA Standards to the Virtual Reference Interview," *Reference & User Services Quarterly* 54, no. 1 (September 25, 2014): 8–11, doi: 10.5860/rusq.54n1.8.
4. Judith Logan et al., "Dissatisfaction in Chat Reference Users: A Transcript Analysis Study," *College & Research Libraries* 80, no. 7 (November 2019): 925–44, doi: 10.5860/crl.80.7.925.

A GENEALOGY LIBRARY IN THE PANDEMIC AGE

— Cheryl A. Lang —

A genealogy library and its librarians know how to dig deep for answers, but when the COVID-19 quarantine hit in March 2020, flexibility and creativity became more of a priority. Shutting down the library to customers was completed in just two days, and both staff and management were scrambling to figure out how to keep meeting customers' needs.

The Midwest Genealogy Center (MGC) located in Independence, Missouri, is part of the Mid-Continent Public Library (MCPL), the largest library system in Missouri. The MGC is one of the United States' preeminent resources for family history, and its collections offer resources for genealogical research that spans the United States and countries around the world. The MGC also houses a uniquely expansive circulating collection and almost completely open stacks as well as access to databases, scanning and digitization stations, oral history recording kits, microfilm reader scanners, and more.

THE QUARANTINE

Beginning in mid-March 2020, the entire library system was shut down completely to the public and staff in order to quarantine for nine weeks. The first step of this quarantine was organization of the full- and part-time staff to work from home, and keeping them informed, equipped, and available to continue the mission of helping people find their family history. During those nine weeks, the staff responded to queries that could be answered without physical library resources and replied to the other queries that a response would be made after the library reopened. Because all in-person classes had been canceled, MGC staff began creating short videos for our website of what they would have been teaching: Beginning Genealogy, Using Fold3, and Census Research (www.mymcpl.org/genealogy/get-started/online-learning). When Ancestry.com began providing free remote access to customers of any library system with an Ancestry Library Edition subscription, the number of e-mailed questions on how to search grew, and our staff were able to still help those customers.

With the MGC staff chomping at the bit to keep busy, work-at-home indexing and imaging editing of previous scanning projects were added to the staff's duties. Regular communication between all staff and the MGC managers began with a steep learning curve when it came to online videos, however. Creating and joining Microsoft Teams meetings, and coordinating meetings with forty staff members in forty different places, took some initial mastering of the technology, but keeping in touch, seeing each other's faces, and laughing at screen backgrounds were important to maintain the library's teamwork and staff bonding.

PHASED REOPENING

The MCPL administration, coordinating plans with local health departments and the Centers for Disease Control and Prevention's (CDC's) recommendations, began a phased reopening plan at the end of May 2020 that involved the ordering of personal protective equipment, the redistribution of the staff's work areas to maintain social distancing, and sanitizing the building. Initially, only staff were allowed in the building for the first few weeks, and the first direct service to be provided to customers was restricted to curbside pickup and the delivery of books. About 10 percent of the genealogy print resources were available for checkout, so customers were still able to do some research by placing holds on and picking up books. MCPL had also made the decision to forgive all fines from the closing in March through the end of June, and with the return of curbside pickups, books began to find their way back to the library. In accordance with the CDC guidelines and studies on the time the coronavirus could live on books, the library administration implemented a system-wide quarantine of returned materials; at first the quarantine period was for three days, but later it became five days, as more data became available.

Tracing logs for staff were initiated—name, verification that they had no new symptoms or were ill before coming into work, their time in and out

FIGURE 4.1 | The Midwest Genealogy Center posted signs alerting visitors that face masks were mandatory.

Face masks are required inside this branch.	Se requiere una máscara facial dentro de la biblioteca
All customers must comply with the Kansas City Health Department's mandate unless you qualify for a specific exemption.	Todos los clientes deben cumplir con el mandato de Kansas City Health Department a menos que usted califique para una exención específica.
VISIT MYMCPL.ORG/COVID FOR UPDATED INFORMATION	VISITE MYMCPL.ORG/COVID PARA OBTENER INFORMACION ACTUALIZADA.

of the building, and where in the building they had worked. Even small changes became important: after days of sanitizing the writing implements used between staff and customers, the library purchased retractable pens that could be attached to each staff member's lanyard for their sole use, and golf pencils used by customers were then given to them to keep.

In the next phase of the reopening plan, customers were allowed in the building, primarily to use its technical services: computers, copiers, and scanners. State and local executive orders on occupancy levels and mask requirements were in place by this time, so when the library did reopen to customers, the decreased building capacity helped people maintain social distancing. Overall, most customers did wear masks voluntarily, and the library provided masks to those who didn't have one with them. Building alterations included adding foot pulls to the restroom doors, cordoning off the stacks from the public, and sanitizing between each customer who used a computer or table space.

CURRENT AND FUTURE LOOK OF THE GENEALOGY LIBRARY

As social distancing and pandemic-reduction measures continued through the year, many people who were staying home found time to either start on or continue working on finding their family history. To help reduce cross-contamination, the open book stacks have been closed to customers. But because the MGC's focus is primarily research, customers can come into the library, request as many as ten books at a time, and staff retrieve those books and enable customers to do their research. An interesting observation has been made on how our reference service has moved backward in time from open shelves to the "reading rooms" of the library past!

One service the MGC staff has certainly found to be on the increase is consultative appointments; especially when beginning their family history journey, people have a lot of questions to ask us. Making appointments to talk one-on-one with a genealogy librarian, and utilizing Zoom or Microsoft Teams to do it virtually, has allowed us to continue that personal touch which both our customers and staff had missed. Another genealogy library service that has seen a huge increase is e-mailed or chat queries: "I see you own this or that book and I need a copy of the index, looking for the names Johnson or Jones," or "How do I find a naturalization record for my immigrant ancestor?" Amateur genealogists know that librarians are the people they should turn to to find the answers to these questions, and they will utilize any available communication avenue to ask those questions.

For the future, there has been much conversation about "returning to normal" or "the new normal," but MGC staff have simply adjusted to the pandemic changes and are moving forward in their mission to serve genealogy customers. Helping people find their family history is just what genealogy librarians do, and a COVID-19 pandemic won't stop them. Mention a death date in 1918, and every genealogy librarian will instantly tell you the death was likely either from World War I or the Spanish flu pandemic. The global pandemic from over a century ago is suddenly very relatable now. Those photographs of people in face coverings and the statistics of infection and death rates are part of the world as we know it now.

REFLECTIONS

Pandemic time in a genealogy library has been very much like a "major life change" for a person. For instance, a marriage or divorce, illness, or a death in the family changes a person's lifestyle, mindset, and how they view things, but life still goes on. The pandemic experience has been life-changing for the staff of the Midwest Genealogy Center, and it has been interesting to examine and compare our thoughts and feelings on how things have changed. One major change is how curbside service is now a "norm," but why wasn't that service offered before? Some newer library buildings have drive-up windows for pickup, but for most buildings, why did we insist on making customers walk into the library to pick up materials? Would it not have been excellent customer service (before the pandemic) to walk to the front door and deliver those books on hold to waiting customers?

The same could be said of Zoom one-on-one consultations. In-person, sit-down appointments were the norm before this year, but they are fewer and more difficult now. To mitigate virus transmission, limitations on the time customers can come into the library, whether customers want to come in at all, and requirements for face masks have changed in-person reference transactions. Using online video for these consultations could have been a service in place before the pandemic. What other tools and methods have not yet been considered to connect with the MGC's customers? The COVID-19 pandemic has provided a unique opportunity for genealogy librarians to find other ways to help people find their family history.

HOTSPOT LENDING
DURING A PANDEMIC

— Suzanne Wulf —

Before the pandemic and global shutdown, I believed the Niles-Maine District Library (where I am the head of Digital Services) was adequately meeting the technology needs of our users and lessening the digital divide. During the past decade as society moved online, the library made a concerted effort to improve access to technology and increase digital literacy in our community. We offered regular technology classes, opened a media lab, circulated technology equipment, and provided access to desktop computers and laptops, with staff available to assist users. However, the COVID-19 pandemic revealed that a significant portion of our district is without broadband internet at home and had limited or no internet access when the library closed. When the pandemic started, the hotspot lending program we already had in place unexpectedly became a lifeline for some users to connect socially, research health information, order groceries, and participate in remote learning. Our hotspot program was able to bridge various gaps by providing the means for users to get online.

NILES HOTSPOT PROGRAM

Libraries are access-centric institutions that have mastered the logistics of lending materials. Loaning out technology equipment is an extension of the circulation services we already have in place with a few small differences. Niles-Maine District Library is a suburban library district located just north of Chicago that serves approximately 57,000 people. The district is a diverse community with varying levels of digital literacy. Several years ago, we identified a need in the community for access to broadband internet after tracking the demand for our public computers. The library started circulating hotspot devices in 2015 after seeing the success other libraries were having with similar programs. Our hotspot lending program aligned with our strategic goals and was a way to expand our library services outside of the building.

Working with Mobile Beacon, we started our hotspot lending program in 2015 with five devices and gradually increased their number over time. We now have seventeen devices available for circulation for a three-week loan period. We purchase hotspot devices at a one-time cost of $60–70, depending on the devices available. The annual service plan for unlimited data costs about $120 per device.

PANDEMIC HOTSPOT USERS

When the library shut down in March 2020, users had checked out 15 of the 17 devices. The typical three-week loan period was extended through the end of July, when we began accepting materials back into the building. I interviewed a number of the patrons who had devices checked out during this time to understand their needs and use of the hotspots.

One patron checked out a hotspot for his elderly mother to use with an older iPad. He wanted to keep her connected in a cost-effective way, and the library hotspot was a good solution. He appreciated that the device is very simple to use, and he can easily troubleshoot it himself or call the library for assistance. Another hotspot user is a retired woman who typically uses her smartphone as a hotspot, but her phone plan limits the amount of content she can stream or download. When she purchased a new iPad Pro, she was not interested in procuring broadband internet at home due to her fixed income.

One middle-aged patron didn't have any access to the internet aside from the hotspot device he had obtained from the library. He was using the hotspot to find the latest information about the COVID-19 virus. When I spoke to him about returning the device, I could sense his rising panic. He was fearful about not being able to access current information about the virus, and he asked to be added to the waiting list for the next available device.

Our hotspot users ranged in age. For example, there was a young man who didn't have broadband internet at home because the plans were too expensive. He lives with roommates, and they would take turns streaming from their phones if they didn't have a hotspot to use. A common trend among all of these users—young and old alike—was that they didn't view broadband internet as a worthwhile investment. Before the pandemic struck, there were ample places in the community to get online; and other users just considered the cost of buying and using a hotspot device to be prohibitive.

LESSONS LEARNED

Educating our community about affordable internet access options has emerged as a strategic goal since the shutdown began. The Bridging the Gap program, which is offered through a partnership between Mobile Beacon and PCs for People, provides internet access for individuals and families living below the poverty line. Libraries can sign up to be a partner in this program, and qualified patrons can register to get broadband internet at a significantly reduced rate. We have also begun researching the number of households in our district without broadband internet access at home in order to reach these users.

The reality is that we don't have nearly enough hotspot devices to allow patrons to keep them out indefinitely, and the devices need to be returned to fulfill existing holds. If a device is not returned, we work with Mobile Beacon to disable the data to that device. Initially, we had issues getting some of the devices returned. I called and spoke with these patrons to assure them they would be in the queue for the next available hotspot; they returned the devices within a few days. It is a difficult decision to block data during these challenging times, but if a device is significantly overdue, we have to disable access due to demand. Another issue affecting our collection is the quarantine period for returned devices. We have modified our policy to allow patrons to return hotspots in the book drop because the devices are packaged in hard-shell cases. However, the time in quarantine has recently increased to seven days and is significantly hampering our ability to turn over the devices to the next patron.

Since the shutdown happened so quickly and with very little warning, it was critical that our hotspot collection was in good, working condition and none of the devices were waiting to be repaired. I highly recommend developing a workflow for handling damaged and defective devices. Here are some suggestions for practices that have worked well at our library:

- Create a list of troubleshooting tips for staff to perform before a hotspot device is marked for repair. The staff might be able to solve the problem on their own.
- Assign and train at least two staff members to handle non-working devices.

- Establish a reasonable time period for repairs to be completed.
- Keep an up-to-date hotspot inventory with each device's bar code, device type, MEID or serial number, and circulation or repair status.
- Keep an extra stock of batteries, chargers, and cases on hand in order to quickly swap out broken parts.

BROADBAND IS MORE IMPORTANT THAN EVER

The COVID-19 pandemic has confirmed how essential broadband internet access is for all communities. Imagine how different your life would be if you couldn't connect with your family, friends, or colleagues, and you didn't have access to accurate information about the virus during the shutdown. So many of us, myself included, take for granted having easy access to broadband internet. But there are quite a few people in our communities who don't have such access, for one reason or another. Some perceive hotspot lending as a niche service for libraries, but this is one service that will probably grow in importance over time. If your library is interested in starting a hotspot lending program, there is no better time than right now. The key to success is to customize your program for your library and community. With numerous libraries launching hotspot lending programs, there is a strong network to help troubleshoot any issues you might encounter.

Hotspot How-to Resources

Are you looking to build a hotspot lending program at your library? Check out these online guides and webinars:

DigitalLead: Hotspot Lending at Your Library
www.ala.org/pla/education/onlinelearning/webinars/ondemand/hotspots

Starting a Mobile Hotspot Lending Program
www.maine.gov/msl/libs/tech/How-to-Hotspot.pdf

DigitalLead: Rural Libraries Creating New Possibilities
www.ala.org/pla/initiatives/digitallead/hotspot-playbook

PLA Hotspot Resources
www.ala.org/pla/sites/ala.org.pla/files/content/onlinelearning/webinars/
archive/PLA-Hotspot-Resources_July-22-2019.pdf

MOVING HEALTH AND WELLNESS ONLINE AT YOUR LIBRARY

— Bobbi L. Newman —

I n recent years we have seen many public libraries add health and wellness programs and services to their already robust community offerings. These programs can range from checking out bicycles and snowshoes to patrons, to community educational sessions on end-of-life care, or advice from health care professionals.

When we talk about health and wellness in libraries, I like to use the definition of *health* from the World Health Organization: "Health is a state of complete physical, mental, and social well-being and not merely the absence of disease or infirmity."

Health is more than our physical fitness or the blood stats from our latest doctor visit. Public libraries can improve the mental and social well-being of patrons through a wide variety of programming and services.

MOVING ONLINE

In March 2020, when the COVID-19 pandemic forced libraries to close their physical doors and spaces to the public, many libraries moved their programs online, including programming and services focused on health and wellness. Public library staff used the resources they had on hand, ranging from Zoom to Facebook Live to webcams and smartphone cameras, and turned their living rooms, patios, kitchens, and home offices into stages for programs. They moved all sorts of existing in-person programs online. A number of online programs that bear on health and wellness are described below.

Food and Gardening

The North Scott Plains (NJ) Public Library hosted a cookbook club for in-person attendance for almost six months prior to the pandemic. Members would choose a recipe from the cookbook, make it at home, and then bring their dish into the library for a potluck meal. During the meal, members would discuss the cookbook, including the layout, ease of reading, the ease of finding the ingredients locally, using the suggested techniques for preparation, and the resulting dish. When the library closed its doors in March, the cookbook club was moved online, using options such as an online magazine service to select recipes, or for some meetings just selecting a theme rather than a cookbook.

Health and wellness may not be the first things that come to mind when you think of a cookbook club, but this type of club can be a great introduction to new and healthy foods, as well as seasonal fruits and vegetables and how to prepare them. Additionally, bringing people together for any time of online connection helps increase a sense of community, decreases feelings of isolation and loneliness, and provides a much-needed distraction.

The East Lake Branch of the Birmingham (AL) Public Library launched a Tiny Garden Project as a result of the pandemic. The "Masked Gardener," library staff member James Walker, and other library staff members demonstrate the care of houseplants and vegetable plants while wearing a mask. Patrons are encouraged to start their own container vegetable gardens inside or outside. The Tiny Garden often features recommended books for all ages. Access to fresh produce is an important aspect of health and wellness, and being able to grow your own food is powerful knowledge. Any type of gardening is good for our mental health.

Senior Programs

When the St. Charles Public Library and the Gail Borden Public Library (both in Illinois) closed their doors due to COVID-19, David Kelsey, an outreach services librarian, and Glenna Godinsky, a life enrichment liaison, knew they needed to take their outreach services for seniors online. They worked with the senior centers in their area to ensure that the adults enjoying their programs virtually were following CDC guidelines, including social distancing around the TV or screen, and disinfecting laptops, tablets, and smartphones between each use. The two librarians offer programs in various formats: virtual live programs with hosting software, Facebook Live programs, recorded virtual programs, and audio programs over the telephone.

Among the virtual health programs for seniors are "memory cafés." A memory café is a virtual trip that might include photos, music, sounds, and props related to the region. Memory cafés are helpful for people who have Alzheimer's disease, other forms of dementia, and anyone with mild cognitive impairment. A virtual trip to New Orleans might include screen-sharing of photos of the city, props such as carnival masks, short videos, jazz music, and other sounds of related areas. You can learn more about the program at www.memorycafedirectory.com/. You can also watch a webinar on memory cafés in libraries by Angela Meyers of the Bridges (WI) Library System (https://youtube/KoWEn7GvlRg) or read about the program at the Shrewsbury (MA) Public Library (https://programminglibrarian.org/programs/memory-caf%C3%A9).

Other options for seniors are virtual group coloring, painting, and crafting, which improve dexterity and mental health. Programs held over the telephone include reading poems, short stories, and telling jokes. These programs create a sense of connection and help to combat feelings of loneliness and isolation. Finally, creating mail to send to seniors is a great idea; you can partner with others in the community to draw cards and write letters. You can view the recording of the webinar David and Glenna presented for the Network of the National Library of Medicine at https://youtube/XA0Ec27UuPs.

Children's Programs

Katie Clausen, the early literacy coordinator at the Gail Borden Public Library, took her programming online using her smartphone when her library closed. She hosted a variety of dance parties for children that encouraged movement for physical health and the enjoyment of music and group activities for mental health. One of my favorite programs of hers is the Kindness Storytime, which focused on self-care, care for the earth, and care for others. Other programs, such as homemade obstacle courses, yoga, and meditation, encourage movement and coordination. You can learn more about the technical aspects of Katie's setup in the webinar recording at https://youtube/ufasFHHdBB8.

Virtual programs can also include resources for parents and caregivers. You can invite local specialists to speak about topics such as sleep, day care choices, mental health for children (as well as parents and caregivers), nutrition, and more. Some libraries put together to-go kits for patrons to pick up (following

FIGURE 6.1 | David Kelsey of the St. Charles (IL) Public Library hosts a telephone discussion on 1950s TV western shows.

CDC guidelines) that include a toy or activity for the child to do during the program, allowing the parent or caregiver to focus on the information shared.

PARTNERSHIPS ARE POWERFUL

Many libraries have added virtual programming by partnering with local government, nonprofits, or businesses. Partnerships are a powerful way to expand your offerings without requiring library staff to become experts at everything. Tony Iovino, assistant director of the Oceanside (NY) Library, stressed the importance of creating and maintaining community partnerships as part of a successful move to virtual programming in his April 2020 webinar (https://youtu.be/6EF_TVO3mi0). Consider reaching out to your local health care providers, dentists, hospitals, local colleges and universities, and yoga studios as partners with which to host online programs on health and wellness.

One word of caution about inviting guest speakers offering health advice. There are a growing number of health and wellness promoters who share advice that lacks evidence and, at worst, can even be harmful. Make sure that anyone offering health advice is licensed by a state board in your state.

DON'T FORGET THE STAFF

Many library administrators and managers I spoke with emphasized that in these unprecedented times, even more care needs to be given to the health and wellness of the library's staff. Library staff are not just "working from home"; they are at home trying to work during a pandemic. Caring for and improving the community's health and wellness starts inside the library, with care for the health and wellness of the library's own staff.

There are many aspects to our health—physical well-being, mental health, cognitive health, social well-being, and more. The possibilities for virtual programs that improve the health and wellness of the community are almost endless. Start with something that interests you personally; don't feel that your technology or digital platform needs to be perfect; don't be afraid to learn from what works, and throw away what doesn't work.

Even More Health and Wellness Virtual Programming Ideas

- Chair tai chi
- Yoga or chair yoga
- Overcoming stress and anxiety through meditation
- Beginner tai chi
- Regrowing your veggies: Edible recycling
- Anti-loneliness chats
- Drop by and chat
- Parent and caregiver mixer
- TED Talk viewing and discussions
- TV show discussions
- Social hours
- Coloring
- Arts and crafts
- DJ dance party
- Book chats
- Guest speakers/presenters
- Cooking
- Gardening
- Lectures
- Trivia
- Poetry
- Words with friends
- TikTok challenge: Videos of dancing, chores, obstacle courses
- Finding reliable health information online

COMMUNITY CAN
HAPPEN ANYWHERE

— Kate Hall and Christophe Andersen —

Northbrook is a suburb about 25 miles north of Chicago with a population of about 33,000. The Northbrook Public Library boasts a beautiful 87,000-square-foot building and has more than 100 staff members. Our community appreciates us, and our tagline says it all: we are the place "Where Community Happens."

On March 12, 2020, we made the tough call to close the library to patrons and transition the staff to remote work. March 13, 2020, was our last day open to the public. We didn't know it at the time, but we would not see patrons in person again until July 20, 2020. As we closed the building, we wondered what new ways we would have to dream up to continue to be the place "Where Community Happens."

As we worked on transitioning the staff to remote work, we quickly pivoted to providing virtual services to our patrons, but this meant that we needed to be able to offer library cards.

LIBRARY CARDS

Libraries are public spaces, and we happily welcome patrons from anywhere into the physical building. We pride ourselves on being open to all members of the public. But what do you do when you don't have a physical place for people to gather? As the shutdown began, we ramped up our virtual offerings ranging from programs to databases, as well as downloadables.

In order to access those services, though, people needed a library card. We have a solid cardholder rate of over 70 percent, but what about those people who didn't have cards or who lived in unincorporated areas? Should the same rules apply for our residents in unincorporated areas? We felt that we needed to be generous in offering services to everyone who lived in town, and the Illinois State Library agreed and relaxed the rules around non-resident cards.

In Illinois, about 10 percent of the population lives in unincorporated areas and does not pay property taxes to their local library. In order to receive service, they have to pay an annual amount based on their tax bill or based on a per capita sum. In and around Northbrook we have pockets of non-residents, many with children, who now had no way to access our resources. So we worked out a plan to give these non-residents library cards.

We started by setting up an online application form on our website (www .northbrook.info/visit/use/temporary-library-card). We gathered the basic information we needed to give people a card:

- Name
- Birthday
- Parent/Guardian Name (if under 18)
- Address
- E-mail Address
- Phone

Once the form was filled out on our website, our circulation staff reviewed the information to make sure a card was not already in existence, and then they e-mailed the new cardholder their card number and a clue to their PIN number. We set the cards' expiration dates at sixty days to start with, since we didn't know how long the building would be closed.

With their new cards, patrons could immediately start downloading our e-resources and using our online databases. The compliments flooded in. We filled over 200 cards in the first couple of weeks.

Some people might argue that we didn't do the proper vetting to make sure the applicants were actually Northbrook residents, and were giving cards to people who lived in unincorporated areas, but we saw it differently. We are still in the midst of a global crisis. Libraries are there to connect people with information. Normally, anyone can walk through the doors and access the treasure trove of information found in your average public library. But that isn't possible right now. We have a duty to our communities and our country to help people get through this time. And what we can do is give people a library card, even if they live in an unincorporated area.

HOMEBOUND SERVICE

Once we had tackled the library card issue, we turned our attention to other services we could offer our patrons. More than 30 percent of Northbrook's population is over age 65. For many years we had offered a homebound service, and we had 10 or 12 people who used it regularly. But we knew that our most vulnerable population needed us, and there were at least a dozen more people who could use this service.

Our outreach and senior services librarian, Christophe Andersen, thought we could do more with homebound services, but he recognized that the Circulation Department was planning curbside service and couldn't take on the task of expanding homebound service as well. Christophe, along with the rest of the staff in the Fiction and Media Department, said they could handle homebound services, including prepping items and making all the deliveries. We kept it simple and used our existing Homebound web page (www.northbrook.info/visit/use/homebound), while adding a new online application form and using the same scheduling software as the curbside service.

We had no idea how many people to expect. Would it be only a couple? Hundreds? We had to plan for a surge. Multiple staff members, as well as library volunteers, offered to help with the project, and Christophe soon had a game plan worked out, as shown below.

STEPS FOR NEW HOMEBOUND PATRONS

1. Fill out the online application form on our website, or call us to fill it out for you.
2. Wait for a staff member to call and confirm your information, and then put you into our Homebound system.
3. Once verified as a homebound patron, place your holds or have us place them for you.
4. Once you are notified that your holds are available, call or go online to schedule a time for your items to be dropped off.
5. Wait for a call the day of delivery to let you know the window of time we will be dropping off items (usually a one-hour block).
6. Set any items you want to return on your front porch or step.
7. Enjoy your new items!
8. Rinse and repeat as often as once a week.

When first launched, the service did not garner many new people. Had we been mistaken in thinking this was a service our community needed and wanted? But while it took a few weeks, we now have more than thirty-five homebound patrons.

But how does it look from the back end? While we originally intended the service to be largely self-service after enrollment, we soon learned that many patrons needed more assistance. Most of the patrons call us by telephone to place items on hold, some because they aren't comfortable with online technology, and some because they want recommendations on what to read, watch, or listen to next. We also help the patrons with scheduling a delivery time. While this takes more time than we had originally planned, having this type of connection with the patrons allows us to build relationships with elderly people who often have no one else to talk to.

THE STAFF SIDE OF HOMEBOUND SERVICE

1. Items are placed on hold by patrons or staff. Circulation staff pull the items that appear on the picklist just as they would any other hold.
2. Automatic hold notifications (e-mail/text/phone) go out to patrons.
3. The staff help patrons schedule a delivery time.
4. On the day of delivery, the staff pull holds, check out and package items, and arrange the route based on delivery locations.
5. On the day of delivery, the staff call patrons with a specific time window and instructions for returns.
6. The staff deliver items, leaving packages at the front door, apartment lobby, or other location as requested.
7. The staff take returns and then ring the doorbell or call to let patrons know their delivery has arrived.
8. Returns are placed in a bin in the car and brought back to the library for quarantine before being turned over to the Circulation Department.

Because we initially planned for the possibility of up to fifty homebound patrons, we are set up to handle a steady increase of patrons, with other staff ready to assist with item preparation or deliveries. For libraries that don't have access to volunteers to help with this, consider partnering with other local organizations like Meals on Wheels to deliver items. The slow launch of our program provided some favorable opportunities. It gave us time to deliver items to our previous homebound patrons and familiarize them with our new process. And we were able to work with patrons who are new to both the library and the homebound service, getting them library cards and introducing them to our services. The staff also had time to get comfortable with the new procedures, reducing everyone's stress during a challenging time.

And it's working! Our patrons are happy, and the staff have an efficient system that allows for future growth of the service. We view the expanded program as a success and look forward to continuing to serve this vulnerable population.

READY FOR TOMORROW

These are just two of the services we have offered to our patrons during the most challenging time many of us will ever (hopefully) face. Just like libraries around the country, we met our patrons' needs and proved that we could be there for them in new and unique ways. We could be the place where community happens in new and unexpected ways.

Having successfully pivoted at a time when most of us were feeling tremendous stress, we now know that any challenges we face in the future will be met with ingenuity and innovation. We will always be the place where community happens, no matter what the world throws at us.

A NEW READER'S ADVISORY SERVICE DURING THE PANDEMIC

— Paige Knotts, Sarah Lane, and Stephanie Fruhling —

Like most American public libraries, the Des Moines Public Library (DMPL) and its six buildings closed its doors to the public in spring 2020 when the COVID-19 pandemic swept into Iowa.

With a reopening date uncertain and a lack of essential work for the staff, the library leapt into action to create new opportunities and services in order to stay engaged with our patrons. Curbside pickup. Virtual programming. Reallocation of funds and resources to digital materials. This was triage librarianship.

But what was missing was that connection between community and library that had cemented the DMPL's role as a comfort, a resource, a trusted friend, and a curator of patrons' reading journeys. Enter: Book Chat, a new service that arose from the need to meet those human needs of our patrons by offering them choices at a time when locked doors meant they didn't have the traditional ones.

Book Chat (www.dmpl.org/book-chat-lets-find-your-next-great-read) is a dedicated reader's advisory service, with staff at all six branches working to find and collect materials for patrons. By using phone, online, and print channels, our staff has expanded our points of communication to reach our entire community during the pandemic.

THE GENESIS OF A NEW SERVICE

The Des Moines Public Library is the largest public library system in the state of Iowa, with six branches serving the city and surrounding suburbs. After several months of closure due to the COVID-19 pandemic, during which we offered only digital materials and services, the DMPL introduced curbside pickup service in June 2020. Patrons were grateful for access to physical materials again, but they clamored for the discovery and browsing experience. Reader's advisory has long been an integral public service at our library. The library's reference phone lines regularly took calls from patrons asking for book suggestions, or requests for librarians to just choose items for them. It became clear that these patrons' needs were not being met by curbside pickup alone.

We decided we had to expand our reader's advisory staff to become a system-wide team to provide virtual services and more targeted book suggestions. Limited services needn't mean a diminished experience for a patron using a new reader's advisory service. The materials selected, as well as the interaction with the librarian, had to be a rich experience that fulfilled a need not already being met by our expanded digital collections. How could we meet the needs of those patrons who lacked internet access, or who lacked the confidence to find materials without physically browsing in the library building?

We quickly identified the physical limitations of our library buildings as a challenge to moving forward with creating the new service. To do more, we would need more staff, but adding staff during a pandemic had to be done in a way that honored mandated social distancing requirements and safety measures. To solve this problem, we turned some study rooms into offices. We built workflows online through Sharepoint so our staff could access them from home. We created a manual so that the staff at any branch could contribute to the work.

READER'S ADVISORY SERVICE GOES REMOTE

Departments and staff across the library system quickly collaborated to build the new service. The reader's advisory team had already laid the groundwork for translating traditional services to the virtual space. In-person reader's advisory interviews could be moved to the phone; patrons would be able to call a new hotline, answer some questions about their preferences, and the library would then put together a list of suggested titles in just a few days. And equally importantly, patrons would now be able to fill out a form on the DMPL's website in which they indicated their preferences, and then the reader's advisory librarians would suggest a list of recommended titles. With either the telephone or the online service, the library could put the titles it recommended on hold for curbside pickup by the patron. Now it was time to formalize these new services under a new identity to share with the public.

The library's community engagement team built a website, logos, and offered valuable branding feedback on an initial plan within twenty-four hours. A web form, inspired by peer libraries, was drafted and approved (www.dmpl .org/book-chat-form). Patrons could now share their reading habits and interests, and the Book Chat team of librarians would provide book suggestions in return.

Book Chat was born. After an incredible amount of communication and organization, Book Chat soft-launched on July 20, just a few weeks after we met for the first time as a team following the staff furloughs.

Patrons with internet access can now fill out the form on our website and receive a list of suggested titles in just a few days. The library can then put those titles on hold for curbside pickup. Patrons can also call our new Book Chat live hotline to have a conversation about books they might enjoy, or just dictate the exact titles they're hoping to read. We receive more online submissions than calls, but access to librarians should not be limited to those with internet access.

The telephone hotline is staffed Monday through Friday, from 10:00 a.m. to 5:00 p.m. Patrons can call the number directly, or they can be transferred by the system's telephone reference staff. This was designed in part to ease the burden of calls for the telephone reference staff, who take as many as twenty-five calls each hour while the library is closed, and don't have the time and ability to hold a readers' advisory interview with a caller.

All requests, regardless of how the question is received, go to a shared e-mail. A team member is assigned to check the e-mails during the week and assign requests to Book Chat staff. We do this on a rotating basis and are able to organize assignments and workflows through a shared log. All six branches work to provide personalized book suggestions to patrons within 3–5 days, and to fulfill Book Bundle requests within one business day. (See below.) The staff complete these tasks in addition to supporting our curbside pickup services.

The library's community engagement team implemented a marketing strategy to promote the new service to the community, with a limited launch on our website and social media (before doing a full promotional rollout two weeks later). This delay was intended to give the Book Chat team a chance to see the types of requests coming in and test the workflow process.

Book Chat by the Numbers

An Average Week for Book Chat

- 18 Book Chat requests
- 6 branches fulfilling requests and suggesting titles
- 45 minutes per request to find personalized suggestions tailored to each patron
- 3–5 day turnaround
- 67 percent adult materials requests
- 33 percent youth materials requests

We soon identified another community need—the "please, just grab anything and help me get some books that aren't *Cat in the Hat*" requests from parents—and so we added a second web form for this sort of request. Then the Book Chat staff put together a "bundle" of five books for the child (or children), and these Book Bundles are available for pickup within one business day. The bundles are extremely popular, with one family calling them Christmas with books! Patrons enjoy the convenience and surprise of having items pre-selected for them.

TEAMWORK MAKES THE BOOK CHAT DREAM WORK

The response from the community to Book Chat was swift and positive, but we quickly found ways to tweak and improve the service. The management at two branches saw a need for Book Bundles for adults, so this age group was added to the web form. Many initial requests were for books for teens, so we updated the Book Bundle web form again to include options for chapter books and young adult materials.

On our Book Chat hotline, patrons requested travel books that listed lodging options, while another patron asked for beginning exercise books for seniors that had clear pictures. These are materials that would normally be found by browsing the shelves and looking through individual books. We knew these requests would take extra time, so our staff schedules were adjusted.

We created instructional documents outlining staff responsibilities, schedules, and workflows, all housed on our Microsoft Teams page and shared with the Book Chat team. Over the following weeks, as more staff became involved, we continued to update these documents, eventually creating an online Book Chat manual.

Communication is key but is an extra challenge when working with staff and managers in six different buildings. Our Microsoft Teams page is the main hub for communicating information to one another, but we regularly check in with staff to see how things are going and ask for feedback and suggestions. The staff might not always volunteer information; we learned a lot by simply *asking.*

Reader's advisory training is another important piece of the puzzle. An online workshop with the reader' advisory specialist Becky Spratford helped our Book Chat team get up and running, and we added additional training resources to our Microsoft Teams page. Although most of our staff members are happy to suggest books, their experience and comfort levels vary. These trainings were crucial in connecting team members to each other and building a culture where the staff support each other and feel comfortable admitting that they need help with certain requests.

While the logistical demands of this service are challenging and necessary to address in order to ensure that requests are promptly filled, it's the nuances of each interaction that influence how we select items and how we'll tailor additions to this program in the future (yes, we've already got more plans).

Our patrons' requests aren't limited to favorite genre designations. The requests are as much for connecting and exploring ideas as they are for singular titles. Our statistics show the rate at which we fulfill requests, but we're placing just as much emphasis on the feedback we receive from patrons. We know they find this service comforting because they thank us for helping them endure the pandemic. We know we're trusted because they share their personal reading habits and preferences with us so we can help them find more materials. And we know they identify us as their reading curators because they've asked for subscription services.

Our staff continue to innovate and brainstorm new additions for this service. With their passion to serve paired with our community's enthusiasm to read, we're confident we'll continue finding success with Book Chat.

IMPROVING ACCESSIBILITY IN VIRTUAL PROGRAMS AND SERVICES

— Carrie Banks and Barbara Klipper —

W hen the COVID-19 pandemic limited service and closed buildings, libraries were forced to reexamine their programs and services, including those for people with disabilities. One solution was to bring the programming online. Some libraries already had virtual programming for people with disabilities, like the San Francisco Public Library's series "American Culture: The Deaf Perspective," a four-part, captioned, English/ASL video exploring Deaf heritage, folklore, literature, and diversity.[1]

Other libraries quickly followed suit and offered online versions of programming that serves people with disabilities. Jen Taggart, at the Bloomfield (MI) Township Public Library, filmed her library's adaptive storytime, captioning the video for accessibility. The Skokie (IL) Public Library brought its "Rainbow Therapy Time" dog program to Zoom. They enhanced accessibility for viewers by sending out a list of keywords they could use to practice saying or program into communication devices.

Other libraries created new content. For example, Renee Grassi of the Dakota County (MN) Library and Alex, a person with autism who is also a former library volunteer and current library school student, co-created "All About Autism," an inclusive storytime for children incorporating strategies from Sensory Storytime, and hosted it on Facebook Live.

WHAT IS VIRTUAL ACCESSIBILITY?

To some extent, the above programs were made accessible because they were designed for people with disabilities. However, *all* virtual library programs should be made accessible, since accessible programs are naturally inclusive, welcoming everyone. It is also easier to create accessible programs than to adapt inaccessible ones later when access is requested. For this reason, one of the last projects of the Association for Specialized, Government, and Cooperative Library Associations as an ALA division was the Virtual Accessibility Toolkit. Created by the Accessibility Assembly, it is available on the Reference & User Services Association's website.[2] Some highlights of the toolkit follow.

Universal Design for Learning

Universal Design for Learning (UDL) principles can help us create virtual programs that are equitable and available to people of all abilities.[3] The three UDL principles are:

1. Multiple means of engagement
2. Multiple means of presentation
3. Multiple means of action and expression

Miss Rachel's virtual Sensory Storytime for the William James Memorial Library in Lafayette Hill, Pennsylvania (https://bit.ly/2En9XWq), applies UDL principles in many ways, including:

Multiple means of engagement:
- having a simple background helps viewers focus on the presenter and the activities
- pacing that allows time for viewers to process the content, and also allows occasional downtime
- incorporating thought prompts like "if you guessed"

Multiple means of presentation:
- including movement activities and songs

Multiple means of action and expression:
- reading a bilingual story
- using readily available items, like rice-filled bottles for shakers and dish soap for bubbles, thereby facilitating participation by people from varied economic backgrounds

Platform Accessibility

Software and platform accessibility are equally critical to program access. Zoom, WebEx, and Google Meets, the preferred platforms for many libraries, have the following advantages:

- compatibility with the most adaptive technology (AT)
- phone participation options
- capabilities for captioning and chat

Each of these platforms has its own strengths and weaknesses. WebEx allows for renaming on the phone. According to Kaitlyn Hodges, the Bayside (VA) Special Services Library's disability services librarian, Zoom and WebEx interact well enough with AT to allow moderators who are blind or have low vision to conduct programs. The interface between Google Meets and Macs has been found to be cumbersome at best for presenters using AT, but Google Meets provides good computer-generated captions without extra charge.

Phone Access

For many people, dialing in is their only, best, or most comfortable way to access library programs. Popular phone programs include:

- The Brooklyn Public Library's "Dial a Story or Poem," which brings new content to patrons daily; and its Inclusive Services Department's "Navigating Disabilities System, One to One Assistance," which arranges phone appointments with navigators from the library's partner agency, INCLUDEnyc.
- The Deerfield (IL) Public Library's "Library Lifeline," a program of "one-to-ones and check-ins for older adults and adults with developmental or physical disabilities . . . [offering] basic reference assistance, help accessing e-materials . . . and just . . . a friendly voice on the phone."
- The Ohio Library for the Blind and Physically Disabled and other libraries offer technology assistance by phone to persons with disabilities.

Telephone programs, which bypass the barriers of other platforms, can be lifelines, and people who are Deaf and those with speech disabilities can use 711, the national relay service, to participate in them. Jill Rothstein, the chief librarian at the Andre Heiskell Braille and Talking Book Library, said that when her staff called people they had not heard from, "people were so appreciative of that kind of contact when they have not been able to have other kinds of contact right now. That's very important."

Visual and Auditory Supports

Captions enhance access for people who are Deaf or who have hearing impairments, as well as some people with auditory-processing disorders and learning disabilities. You will probably have to pay for captioning, but it's worth it for the expanded audience and goodwill it provides. Where captions are automatically generated, like on YouTube or Google Meets, remember to edit them. On a related note, remember that streaming content should be caption-enabled.

Open captioning or ASL (American Sign Language) interpretation has been slow to come to libraries. At the very least, it must be available by request as part of your reasonable accommodations. The Brooklyn Public Library brought ASL interpretation online with its "Brainy Babies" program, an early literacy program for infants, toddlers, and caregivers in a low-income community. One poll showed that the "ASL Word of the Day" was the favorite program segment of almost half of all the participants.

Describing visuals expands access to patrons who are blind, those who struggle with social cues, and those participating by phone. Having people say their name before they speak and making sure at least some streaming movies have audio descriptions also contribute to accessibility.

TEACHING PEOPLE TO USE VIRTUAL SERVICES

When the pandemic hit, virtual platforms were new to many library users. Since the member libraries of the Library of Congress's Library Service for the Blind and Physically Handicapped had always taught people how to use technology as part of their mission, as programs went virtual, so did their teaching. Jill Rothstein at the Andrew Heiskell Library believes that these technology training programs are the most important programs her library has done:

> [These programs] are engaging people who are more isolated than they have ever been, in a time when everyone is relying on digital and there is a huge digital divide . . . We are relying on programming to help solve the current problem by teaching them how to use all these digital resources. We are doing something to address the digital divide.

Through individual coaching and monthly meetings of four or five people, these programs teach patrons with print disabilities to use the hardware, software, and platforms needed to access virtual programs and services. Remember, virtual programs are not accessible unless people know how to use them! You can also improve accessibility by reminding your audience at the beginning of each program about features like captioning and by describing community accessibility standards, like muting yourself when not speaking and announcing yourself when speaking.

Attention and Focus

Staying focused on a program can be problematic for some people with learning and attention issues, mental health issues, developmental disabilities, and dementia. Visual schedules can help them anticipate what's next and follow along, decreasing their anxiety.

Busy visual or musical backgrounds can also distract or overwhelm people. Virtual backgrounds can create other barriers. Body parts sometimes disappear into virtual backgrounds, which can be triggering for some audience members. Having multiple things going on at once can also be stressful and distracting. Since you want people to follow the main content, you should use music only as the lead-up to a Zoom meeting, as a program component, or as an entire program, like the Brooklyn Public Library's autism-friendly concerts for all ages. Each autism-friendly Zoom concert offers a social story in advance and has a visual schedule as a banner. Participation, using household items such as pencils and pots, is encouraged during conducting and percussion times. The programs are social, and the movement and banners provide sensory tools for self-regulation. To find out about future concerts, go to www.musicforautism.org.

MAKING CONNECTIONS

Accessible programs don't just enable contact and connection for patrons. By using Google Hangouts to read, discuss, and recommend poetry for their online "Poetry Time," the staff of the Andrew Heiskell Library's branches found they were able to collaborate more easily than ever. "Seeing Beyond," a program of the Bayside Special Services Library and the Virginia Beach

---

Learn More

Virtual Accessibility Toolkit
- Reference & Users Services Association
  www.ala.org/rusa/virtual-accessibility

Virtual Storytime Services Guide
- Association for Library Services to Children
  www.ala.org/alsc/virtual-storytime-services-resource-guide

Digital Accessibility Resources and Guidelines
- NYC Mayor's Office for People with Disabilities
  www1.nyc.gov/site/mopd/resources/digital-accessibility-guides.page

Accessible Video Calls
- Rooted in Rights
  https://rootedinrights.org/video/accessible-video-calls/

Public Library, held a Juneteenth celebration in the middle of the Black Lives Matter movement. It included a presentation, local oral histories, and chat. According to the disability services librarian Kaitlyn Hodges, the celebration generated support for both the library and the African American Cultural Center and brought the two communities together.

Building a new model from the ground up allows us to get it right the first time, developing programs and services that everyone can participate in, learn from, and enjoy. Virtual accessibility can help us turn this period of restricted access to brick-and-mortar libraries into one of wider library usage by welcoming new, often-neglected audiences. It is up to us to seize the opportunity and create something wonderful.

NOTES

1. San Francisco Public Library, https://sfpl.org/locations/main-library/deaf-services/american-culture-deaf-perspective.
2. Virtual Accessibility Toolkit: www.ala.org/rusa/virtual-accessibility.
3. For more information about the Universal Design for Learning, go to www.cast.org/impact/universal-design-for-learning-udl.

STORYTIME IN THE
SUMMER OF COVID-19

— Suzanne DeKeyzer James —

T he staff of the Bienville Parish Library in Louisiana began hearing reports of an illness in China in early January 2020, and then by mid-February there were reports of illnesses in Washington state nursing homes. We were already beginning to consider what we should do with an upcoming children's event on March 6. However, with the guidelines we had at the time, we decided to move forward with hosting our programs, though we reduced the number of participants for senior-adult programming, since they appeared to be the group most vulnerable.

"Seussical the Musical" was to be our last children's event to host. On the day of the program, we were bursting at the seams with more than 1,000 children, teachers, parents, and chaperones, as well as library staff, in a local events center. Exhausted but pleased with the turnout, we returned to the library only to learn that the performer scheduled for an adult program on March 13 was canceling due to health concerns. At that moment, we realized something serious was coming our way. On March 18, the Bienville Parish Library closed.

STAYING CONNECTED

The issue of how to stay connected to our patrons led us to social media. We already had a library Facebook page and branch group pages, so these became the first line of contact to our adult patrons and their children. We encouraged the exploration of our online resources so that children could sample what was available. Patrons with book requests or questions could

---

Two Weeks of Change: A COVID-19 Timeline

- March 9, 2020: First reported COVID-19 case in Louisiana
- March 13, 2020: Public schools in Louisiana closed
- March 18, 2020: The Bienville Parish Library closed
- March 23, 2020: Louisiana Governor John Bel Edwards issued a statewide stay-at-home order

---

reach us through Facebook Messenger. In-person performers were canceled, and the governor's extended order restricted no more than twenty-five people in a public building. Children's Librarian Cheryl Hough, along with the library administration, settled on the solution: we needed to go virtual.

GOING VIRTUAL

Other libraries around the state were doing live storytime sessions via Facebook, and we watched a lot of those sessions looking for ideas. We realized that the main ingredient missing from all of the sessions was—an audience. Having an audience influences the way the storyteller tells the story. In fact, storytelling at its best intimately connects the teller and audience. We needed to somehow re-create the closeness between the storyteller and listeners.

After looking at dozens of exuberant children's librarians telling stories to invisible audiences, we made a list indicating what seemed to be problematic and what we could do differently, and additionally, what worked best for Cheryl Hough. (See table 10.1.)

WORK WITH WHAT YOU HAVE

We found that by keeping things simple, we could produce our own videos that worked for our storytelling purposes. Despite off-camera sounds and falling scenery, we kept going, and the result was a creation that was uniquely different from other libraries' storytime sessions. We know from the positive feedback that the children and adults appreciated our efforts.

Needed Tools

- *Smartphone (Android or iPhone), tablet, or laptop with video capabilities.* We used an iPhone, and the segments filmed were downloaded to our shared drive for editing. Each storytime was saved in a folder, along with the raw footage, music selections, and the finished videos.
- *Tripod for steady filming.* A steady camera is essential and allows for clear, crisp videos.

TABLE 10.1 | Problem/Solution Chart.

Gather your group together for a brainstorming session. List each problem in the left column and begin brainstorming a solution. Remember: No solution is too nutty to dismiss—it just might work. Then get started—overthinking your solutions can only create more problems. Adapt this chart to fit your needs.

PROBLEM	SOLUTION
No audience!	Can't do anything about that; we'll have to pretend. Place the camera as close as possible to Cheryl in the introduction portion of the videos.
Can't see the book; too far away and zooming in and out is distracting.	The book is the focus; create the illusion the child is sitting at Hough's side and reading the story to them.
Uncomfortable being in front of camera and causing nervous flubs.	It will get easier! If there are mistakes, start over and reread the page. Or use them! Kids love it when adults mess up!
No interaction (see problem 1).	Rely on the feedback that comes with Facebook comments and pictures of children posted with their craft projects. Priceless.
How to engage? Keep children and adults interested and coming back each week?	Shout-outs to children and adults. Create a sense of inclusion. Use first and last names—children enjoy hearing their names and the names of their school friends. Add names to the list each week.
What to do with the empty spaces between turning pages and natural pauses?	Place a soundtrack that fits the story or craft project.
Statistics? How to keep track of the number of children/adults?	The number of views and number reached can be counted as a stat.

- *Application for video editing.* Facebook and YouTube have video-editing tools to use. Smartphones also have applications that have nice editing capabilities and are easy to use. We used Adobe Cloud Premiere PRO.
- *A social media platform* to post storytime and craft videos.* What worked best for the library was a Facebook group page, with privacy settings to add an additional layer of protection because there are children watching. The privacy settings allow only invited members to enter the group page. We monitored the page closely and created challenge questions to be answered. If questions went unanswered, the prospective entrants were declined. (*YouTube is another platform with kid-friendly settings.)
- *Optional software.* We used PowerPoint and Adobe Creative Suite.

Helpful Tips

- *Film the introductions and readings separately.* We filmed the introductions and shout-outs before the readings. We had selected books for children from pre-K to age 5, as well as ones for age 6 and up. We framed the opened book so it could be clearly seen, while Cheryl, our presenter, was off-camera reading the story. If you have guest storytellers reading their books, offer to take still camera shots of the book and create a PowerPoint slide-deck. (Don't forget to get their permission.)
- *Music tracks are a plus.* Facebook and YouTube both have a list of royalty-free music loops. We found a very extensive collection of royalty-free music tracks and sound effects from epidemicsound.com (which is ironic and appropriate).
- *Add costumes and other props.* Silly hats, scarves, sock puppets, whatever you might have on hand are great to engage the watching audience. Costumes and props also help leave the adultness behind, so everyone involved can relax and enjoy themselves.
- *Focus on the book.* In many of the storytime videos we viewed, we weren't able to see the book's illustrations clearly. To solve that problem, we filled the video frame with the book so the children were able to see the illustrations and read along.
- *Get as close to the picture book as you can.* If your hands are unsteady, use an easel to prop the book open and turn the pages from the bottom, so your hand and arm don't pass in front of the book.

FIGURE 10.1 | Use empty spaces in the video for messages to your patrons. If something is missed, you can slip in call-to-action phrases as needed.

THAT'S A WRAP!

The takeaway is to be flexible, and remember to have fun! We had our share of technical problems, such as drooping scenery and even an off-screen appearance by a Kansas City Southern Railway train horn!

What occurred to us during the shutdown was how much we needed our patrons and how much they needed us. We had been isolated from one another for months, and when we were finally able to reopen, it was a pleasure just to see our patrons—even from behind a face mask.

There are still restrictions in place, and that is part of our new normal. We will deal with these minor inconveniences and do what we must to keep our patrons and ourselves safe. The summer of COVID-19 was stressful, but even amid social distancing, face masks, and the smell of disinfectant spray, we found that our weekly storytime program was an exciting way to connect to our youngest patrons, with that imaginative response enjoyed only by children at play. And yes—it was fun!

THE GENEALOGY ROADSHOW

Using Partnerships to Enhance Virtual Programming Offerings

— DeeDee Baldwin —

I n early March 2020, as organizations in our state were beginning to shut down against COVID-19, I received a message from Meredith Wickham, the director of the public library in Hernando, Mississippi. She knew that I teach genealogy workshops for the Mississippi State University (MSU) Libraries, and she wanted to see if I would be willing to teach a virtual workshop for the First Regional Library of Hernando. Like many other people in the country, I was anxious and bored, and I welcomed the opportunity to offer one of my favorite workshops.

THE GENEALOGY ROADSHOW

I teach a genealogy workshop, "Branching Out: Starting Your Family Tree with Ancestry.com," at Mississippi State. Like all MSU library workshops, this program is free and open to university students and employees, as well as any interested community members.

The workshop consists of two parts. First, I show patrons how to create a free account on Ancestry.com, set up and navigate their family trees, and use and attach hints. Second, I introduce them to searching records. We go over the most common records they will be using—the Social Security Death Index, census records, draft cards, vital records, and so on—and the search strategies that will yield the most helpful results. Attendees also learn how to use the libraries' subscription to Ancestry.com so they can access records that are not available with a free account.

Chapter 11

The MSU Libraries' coordinator of manuscripts, Jennifer McGillan, teaches an introduction to using the libraries' special collections for genealogy, usually scheduled after my Ancestry workshop. Other colleagues participate in the libararies' annual Templeton Genealogy Fair, a popular event that brings in dozens of community members each June. This has led, in recent years, to nearby public libraries asking us to offer in-person programs for their patrons. Our jokingly nicknamed "Genealogy Roadshow" visited the Winston County Public Library, the Sturgis Public Library, and the Attala County Public Library. Bringing our genealogy instruction to public libraries, then, was already well-established when I was asked to teach a virtual workshop to public library patrons in Hernando.

THE SPRING AND SUMMER OF WEBINARS

Most people will look back on the spring and summer of 2020 as a grid of faces on a Zoom screen. Though many much-anticipated events were canceled, opportunities also arose for people to attend free online events to which they might never have had access otherwise, and libraries worked hard to keep their patrons connected and engaged through creative virtual programming.

An early April date was set for my virtual presentation at the Hernando public library. The library set up the program in Zoom, gave me presenter privileges, and shared the link with patrons on the day of the event in order to prevent Zoom bombing. They created a simple graphic and promoted the event on the library's Facebook page, and I shared it on my Facebook and Twitter pages as well.

I was next contacted by the Columbus-Lowndes Public Library System. I offered the virtual version of my Ancestry workshop to that library's patrons in mid-April. I used MSU's access to WebEx and sent the link to the library to distribute to its patrons. In June I taught a second virtual workshop, "Virtual Cemeteries," in which I showed attendees how to volunteer for and do research on the websites FindAGrave.com and BillionGraves.com. Rounding out the summer, I taught the Ancestry workshop again for another library in late July. Access to the library's Ancestry subscription from home had been extended, and the workshop allowed patrons another chance to learn how to use it.

THE VALUE OF PROGRAMMING PARTNERSHIPS

The value of partnerships between academic and public libraries may seem too obvious to need stating, but it is important to remind ourselves that these opportunities exist. As a land grant university, Mississippi State takes seriously its commitment to serve the public as well as its own students and employees. Offering free programming, both in person and online, is one way to meet those service goals. Virtual programming not only allows a reduction in cost, but (if desired) it can open the webinar to attendees beyond the library's usual patronage, especially with the outreach potential of social media.

Some might wonder about the benefits of offering a program to a local public library when the university library's workshops are already open to the public. While some community members do attend the genealogy workshops held at the university library, many are unaware of these opportunities, and others may not feel comfortable attending educational events (even virtual ones) with college students. Older attendees might feel self-conscious in front of younger adults, especially when computers are involved. Offering these programs through the public library invites an audience that might not have existed otherwise. It also strengthens relationships and encourages networking with colleagues in nearby libraries.

Genealogy programming, in particular, has a variety of benefits. In addition to teaching research skills with the "spoonful of sugar" of a popular hobby, it can raise awareness of libraries' archives and special collections. In her Special Collections workshop, Jennifer McGillan always notes that the archive welcomes donations of family papers, and emphasizes to attendees that their keepsakes will not only be preserved for future generations, but will be used by other researchers instead of gathering dust in an attic.

Many academic libraries also offer workshops on evaluating fake news and the reliability of information found online. If the library has a makerspace, it may offer workshops on popular topics like video editing, 3-D printing, or even sewing.

Public librarians who are interested in connecting with nearby academic libraries for virtual workshops should visit the library's website, where workshops are often listed in calendars or upcoming events. They might also check the website's directory for the contact info of instruction librarian(s) and then e-mail them. Academic librarians should also consider contacting their local public library to offer workshops that might be of interest to their patrons.

At the end of my virtual workshops, I encourage people to e-mail me if they have questions or need help with a genealogical "brick wall." I tell them that genealogy is my obsession and that they would be doing me a favor by asking me to help—and I am only half-joking. My hope is that these connections will lead to future opportunities to partner with public libraries and other organizations.

MOVING THE LIBRARY'S EDUCATIONAL AND CAREER PROGRAMMING ONLINE

— Ashley Welke —

The Pioneer Library System serves Cleveland, McClain, and Pottawatomie Counties in central Oklahoma. With twelve branches and several information stations, we cover approximately 1,900 square miles, with communities ranging from suburban to rural populations. The Pioneer system has a rich history of community-driven programming. Our partnerships are key in understanding the needs of our community, and it is through these relationships that we maximize and deepen our impact. As workforce development has emerged as a priority within our state, Pioneer has worked with several agencies to help align the talent pipeline and close the skills gap. Our recent partnerships include:

- The Central Oklahoma Workforce Innovation Board, to embed a career navigator at our Central branch
- Outreach to the Detention and Correctional Center, emphasizing job skills, literacy, and STEAM
- Connecting local Chambers of Commerce, business professionals, and students as part of the U.S. State Department's Individual Career Academic Planning (ICAP) graduation requirement initiative

PANDEMIC RESPONSE

On March 14, 2020, the Pioneer Library System made the difficult decision to close its buildings to the public. While no one could foresee what was to come, we knew it was critical to continue to meet the needs of our community during this uncertain time. That weekend, our administrative team began implementing our crisis response plans and started identifying ways to provide services in this new environment.

Getting Started

Since we were determined to support our community's learning goals in this rapidly changing environment, Pioneer launched a cross-functional Digital Content Coordinator team three days after closing to the public. Led by a regional coordinator and branch department heads across the system, we identified the following priority areas for digital content:

- Early literacy and school readiness
- STEAM
- Workforce development
- Healthy living
- Literature

These categories were selected to align with corresponding areas identified through our strategic planning process. They are all interconnected and build upon one another; for example, our STEAM programs for children and teens are intentionally designed as career exploration opportunities.

We defined "digital content" as both virtual programs and graphics, and invited the staff at every level to begin creating content. We honestly didn't know what to expect: while we had sporadically produced videos and graphics over the years, this was largely uncharted territory for us. Furthermore, all of our staff were working from home and only had access to personal cell phones and/or computers. But the staff responded resoundingly to the call, and we shared our first digital content through Facebook, Instagram, and YouTube on March 20, 2020. As we checked in with staff, they shared their appreciation for the opportunity to learn new skills, stretch their creative muscles, and most importantly, connect with customers.

Our Initial Process

Before COVID-19, programming and outreach in the Pioneer Library System were primarily developed and implemented at the branch level. Creating digital content to serve our community during the pandemic is probably the biggest system-wide, system-led project we've taken on in terms of staff involvement, scope, and duration. Now that we were operating from one combined perspective, we needed a structure to enhance our collaboration and eliminate duplication. To achieve this, we took the following steps:

- We assigned each content coordinator a specialty area in which they had expertise: early literacy and school readiness, STEAM, workforce development, healthy living, and literature.
- We asked staff to e-mail the appropriate content coordinator when they had an idea for digital content. The content coordinator would provide feedback and connect staff members with one another when similar ideas came forward.
- We asked staff to submit their digital content to a content coordinator once the content had been completed. The content coordinator would assist with editing the content, insert branded intro and outro slides, and then send the content to our Marketing and Communications Department for posting on social media platforms. (As we got more comfortable with digital content, the coordinators began teaching staff how to edit their own videos.)

In addition to implementing this process, we also created a digital content guide for our creators. The guide covered:

- What digital content is, the process for producing it, and how it would be shared
- Tips for creating virtual programs, involving such things as lighting and background, angle and setting up your camera, voice and volume, practicing, copyright, and scripting for the video's beginning and end
- Instructions and embedded videos for video editing
- Tips for creating graphics such as Canva templates, colors, fonts, and placement

To increase consistency between videos, we also developed

- branded intro and outro slides that are used for all virtual programs
- original music that is used at the beginning of all virtual programs

Live Virtual Programs and Presenter Agreements

Initially, all of our virtual programs were recorded and created by the staff. As we geared up for summer, we started digging into how we could offer live virtual programs and contract with the presenters. We chose to use Zoom as our platform for live virtual programs because of its ease of use, general familiarity, and security capabilities. While we had used Zoom internally, to prepare staff to use Zoom in this new capacity, we

- created a guide with links to training videos created by Zoom.
- created a Virtual Branch on our online events calendars. Live virtual programs were added to this calendar so customers could learn about the programs and register for them.

We also contracted with an intellectual property attorney to develop a set of presenter agreements specific to a virtual environment. The result was three agreements that could be used depending on the circumstances: a copyright license agreement, an independent contractor agreement, and a speaker contractor agreement, all geared specifically for library needs.

RESULTS

As of September 1, 2020, the Pioneer staff have created more than 400 videos that have had over 70,000 views. Here are a few examples from our priority areas for digital content:

Early Literacy. Programs designed to build school readiness skills such as fine/gross motor skills, letter/number recognition, staying focused for 10–15 minutes, writing, counting, color and shape awareness, sorting/organizing, and identifying needs and feelings:
- Scheduled storytimes on Tuesdays and Thursdays
- Bilingual Dial-a-Story
- Signing with songs
- Sensory playtime at home

Healthy Living. Programs and graphics designed to improve physical and mental health:
- Nursery rhyme yoga
- How to make the ultimate green smoothie
- Finding exercises you enjoy: the secret to an active lifestyle
- Self-care check-ins: an essential key for navigating difficult times
- Farmscape mindfulness

Literature. Programs and graphics designed to promote literature and discussion and the use of physical materials and digital resources such as OverDrive, Hoopla, and Kanopy:

- Book talks for children, teens, and adults
- Including the very popular for-children-by-children series
- Reading lists and read-alike graphics
- Mayor's book club
- Personalized book recommendations

Workforce Development and Recovery Resources. Programs and graphics designed to build skill sets and to connect employers and job-seekers to critical information:
- Career Online High School, a Gale-Cengage product: this is an online program for adults to earn a high school diploma from an accredited high school
- One-on-one résumé assistance and job-searching
- One-on-one business and career counseling
- Graphics and staff trainings to help patrons understand the Paycheck Protection Program (PPP) and Economic Injury Disaster Loans
- Navigating unemployment
- Database trainings for area Chambers of Commerce, the Oklahoma District office of the U.S. Small Business Administration, and local businesses

STEAM. Programs and graphics designed with discovery in mind to grow the talent pipeline in rising and emerging industries:
- Make your own rocket and exoplanet
- Live concerts
- Smartphone photography
- Programming using Swift and Scratch
- Math and cookies
- LEGO club

In addition, we compiled an extensive live-link list of online learning resources for students that aligns with Oklahoma state standards.

NEW PROGRAMS AND PROJECTS

As we continue to reopen for additional services, Pioneer remains committed to connecting with customers virtually. Here are some new programs and projects that we're working on.

Career Exploration Series

This recorded virtual program series spotlights a variety of Oklahomans in the workforce, from airplane mechanics to small-business owners, with an emphasis on the state's workforce development initiative of 100 Critical Occupations. This series is for teens and adults looking to learn more about career opportunities in our state. It will also align and support our state Department of Education's ICAP graduation requirement.

Virtual Job Fairs

Due to the pandemic, many people have lost their jobs or have seen a significant reduction in hours. At the same time, some industries are expanding and new companies are emerging. Our goal in offering virtual job fairs is to connect job-seekers with employers.

10 to Try

This online reading challenge aims to broaden perspectives by asking community members to read at least ten books selected from the following categories:
1. Author/illustrator of color, different families
2. Book about an Oklahoma historical event
3. Book with a different perspective
4. Book translated into English
5. Book with an LGBTQ character or author
6. Banned book
7. Multicultural folk tale
8. Book involving mental health
9. Book involving diverse abilities
10. Book with a female lead character
11. Book with a refugee character or author
12. Book involving a new holiday or tradition
13. A biography or memoir of a change agent
14. Book involving the body positivity movement

In support of this reading challenge, we plan to have live and recorded virtual programs, including community conversations.

INNOVATIONS TO BENEFIT THE LIBRARY IN THE FUTURE

While we cannot predict when and if our programs will return to pre-COVID levels in terms of delivery, we can continue to meet the needs of our communities in central Oklahoma by doing what we have always done best as pioneers—leveraging our community partnerships and maximizing the talents of our staff to create innovative models that will be of benefit for years to come.

Tips for a Virtual Job Fair

- Start small by reaching out to a select number of employers. Prioritize employers that have multiple job openings, especially those with varied skill and education requirements.
- Publicize your job fair to job-seekers about a month in advance.
- Require registration in order to minimize Zoom bombing and to help prepare job-seekers.
- When sending registrants the link to the event, provide some helpful information about the event:
  - » How to use Zoom
  - » The format (if it is scheduled or is come-and-go), how breakout rooms will be used, how to move from a breakout room into the main room, and how to navigate "lines"
  - » Include helpful tips such as dressing professionally and having a clean, neutral background for the video presentation
- If you can, offer one-on-one appointments for résumé assistance and interview preparation in advance of the job fair.
- During the job fair, assign each employer to a breakout room. Ask employers to log in about forty-five minutes in advance to make sure that everyone is assigned and comfortable using the platform. If possible, assign a staff member to each breakout room to help moderate traffic flow.
- When job-seekers join the virtual event, have a library staff member there to greet them and ask them which employer they would like to speak with. This Zoom host can then move the job-seeker to the corresponding employer's breakout room. When the job-seeker is ready to move on, they simply leave the breakout room and return to the main room to be reassigned.

SERVING OLDER ADULTS DURING A WORLDWIDE PANDEMIC

— *Allan M. Kleiman and Fatima Perkins* —

I n mid-March 2020, faced with a worldwide pandemic, social distancing, and stay-at-home mandates, public libraries across the United States began to close down one by one. Older adults who depended on their local library for in-library browsing, book clubs, and social interaction were suddenly unable to access the services they regularly relied upon.

What are some of the issues that older adults faced when their libraries closed? And what were public libraries' responses in serving older adults during the pandemic?

THREE GENERATIONS OF OLDER ADULTS

It is estimated that 34 percent of the United States population is aged 50 and older. In planning programs and services, many public libraries "lump" adults and older adults into one category. But older adults comprise three distinct generations: Baby Boomers (born 1946–1964), the Silent Generation (born 1925–1945), and the Greatest Generation (born 1910–1924). Despite these three generations' unique characteristics, they all have one thing in common: they are all pre-computer and pre-internet generations. Their members are book readers, newspaper readers, program attendees, library volunteers, and nursing home residents. And they all look to their library for reading material, social engagement, and lifelong learning.

So, given the unprecedented events of the pandemic, how have public libraries continued to serve these generations of older adults? The response of many public libraries was to move from the physical to the virtual. Libraries began to shift gears and go online!

A LIBRARY STEPS UP

At the Montville Township Public Library in northern New Jersey, which was already an "age-friendly" library serving multiple generations of older adults, the strategy was to quickly move programs from in-person to online formats. The first program tested online was the Adult Book Discussion Group, which proved to be a success once the participants learned how to use GoToMeeting. Hoopla was used for the book selection, so participants could simultaneously download and read the book. This was quickly followed online by the popular weekly "Chair Yoga" program, where the median age of the participants is seventy-seven years. Social engagement was added with the weekly Knitting Club, where participants learned to use GoToMeeting with the help of friends, neighbors, and family. Other pieces of the programming puzzle were also moved online, including Tech Talks, which moved to YouTube, and our "Montville U" lifelong learning series. Viewing for the Monday Movies and Friday Foreign Film series was moved to Kanopy. The library offered reader's advisory and tech help to patrons via telephone, e-mail, or GoToMeeting. The library's offerings on Hoopla, Kanopy, OverDrive, RB Digital, Cloud Library, and Creativebug were expanded. Once the library opened for curbside pickup service, bags of crafts materials along with instructions were distributed to older adult patrons to do at home. In addition, the library expanded its Facebook and e-mail communications to all ages of the community to remind them of the virtual services available at the library, in the community, across the country, and around the world.

PROMISING PRACTICES TO ASSIST OLDER ADULTS

The Montville Township Public Library is just one of several libraries that initiated similar commitments to their older adults. Here are some examples of programs and outreach services offered by other public libraries that are suitable to online transition and which show a strong commitment to serving older adults:

- Since mid-April 2020, staffers at the Fort Worth (TX) Public Library have been calling library cardholders over the age of sixty-five to see how they are doing. Recently, the library has taken the extra step of providing "age dementia-friendly library facilities."[1] The Plano (TX) Library has provided a similar service to its older adult patrons.[2]

- The Jefferson County (CO) Library has expanded its call-in-programs, which are done by telephone and allow 100 participants without computers or smartphones to attend programs on the telephone.[3]
- The Springfield-Greene County (MO) Library District expanded its array of virtual programming for older adults and their caregivers. Its programs include the Flying Needles Knitting & Crochet Group, Programs in a Bag, 10 Warning Signs of Alzheimer's, and Exploring Genealogy.[4]
- The Framingham (MA) Public Library developed virtual programs to keep seniors healthy and connected while they are at home, including twice-weekly gentle exercise sessions, several book groups, and Coffee Talk Tuesdays. The library also collected masks in book drops and distributed them to the community and seniors via curbside pickup, distribution events, and by delivery to senior centers.[5]
- The Westerville (OH) Public Library found a way to connect different generations with a pen-pal program. Elementary school-aged children are matched with an older adult who lives in a retirement home, assisted living facility, or nursing home facility. This program builds social skills for the students and reduces the social isolation of the older adult participants.[6]
- The Brooklyn Public Library, a member of the Lifetime Arts Affiliate Network, partnered with a local nonprofit to create a successful virtual art initiative for seniors, Creative Aging Online. The programs are conducted by working, teaching artists.[7]

OLDER ADULTS AND THE DIGITAL DIVIDE

While all of these programs and services developed during the pandemic sound positive, there was a clear challenge in serving older adults: the digital divide. Unfortunately, many "loyal" and "daily" customers who didn't have internet access or a computer were at a loss during the months that libraries were closed. This was especially true for members of the Silent Generation and the Greatest Generation and for those living below the poverty line. A Pew Research study from 2017 indicates that only 4 out of 10 seniors own a smartphone, only 1 in 3 of them own tablets, and just 1 in 5 own an e-reader.[8]

Those with limited computer experience—or no computer experience at all—were now expected to know how to use "Zoom" or learn how to go online to access almost everything a public library had to offer, from virtual programming to e-books. There was clearly more to do. Several libraries developed exciting model programs to address these issues:

- The Elyria (OH) Public Library loaned iPads to the local nursing home so its residents could continue to read online and stay connected with their families during the pandemic.[9]
- The Boston Public Library partnered with local nonprofit organizations to distribute books to Boston's most vulnerable citizens, launching its "Books for Boston" program. The program distributed more than 11,000 books to 22 nonprofit organizations in the Boston area.[10]
- The Boulder (CO) Library Foundation, together with the Boulder Public Library and the Boulder Valley School District, worked together to launch the Boulder Public Library Wifi Hotspot Program, which provided internet access to 225 households in the community.[11]
- The St. Louis County Library designed a program to help customers who need extra technical assistance. Library computer lab assistants provide instruction via e-mail or online. The assistants also provide guidance with the library's e-media materials and more.[12]

Learn More

Libraries Respond: Services to Older Adults
- American Library Association
  www.ala.org/advocacy/diversity/librariesrespond/services-older-adults

Older Populations and Aging
- U.S. Census Bureau
  www.census.gov/topics/population/older-aging.html

Providing Library Senior Services in a COVID-19 World
- Network of the National Library of Medicine
  https://nnlm.gov/class/providing-library-senior-services-covid-19
  -world/25401

LOOKING FORWARD

During the pandemic, public libraries stepped up to the plate, moved their programs and services online, provided services to nursing homes, and distributed books to the vulnerable and the socially isolated. While these were positive steps, issues regarding equity, diversity, inclusion, and accessibility of library services for older adults loom in the background and need to be addressed on a major scale. There is still much more work to be done.

NOTES

1. Fort Worth, "Ft. Worth Public Library Staff Checking in on Senior Patrons," http://fortworthtexas.gov/news/2020/04/COVID-19-Library-Staff-Calling-Seniors/.
2. KRLD.radio.com, "Plano Librarians Make a Difference in the Lives of Isolated Seniors," https://krld.radio.com/articles/news/plano-librarians-make-a-difference-in-the-lives-of-isolated; Mariella Padilla, "Older Adults Remain Isolated Despite Reopening. These Programs Help," *New York Times*, June 8, 2020, www.nytimes.com/2020/06/08/us/coronavirus-elderly-call-outreach.html.
3. Jefferson County Public Library, "Virtual and Call-in Programs," https://jeffcolibrary.bibliocommons.com/events/search/fq=types:(5a13606944fbe2b302340947)?_ga=2.261879182.2035451713.1598409957-2128133638.1598409957.
4. Springfield-Greene County Library District, "Adult Programs," https://thelibrary.org/programs/other/adults.cfm.
5. Framingham Public Library, "Services," https://framinghamlibrary.org/services/seniors/.
6. Westerville Public Library, "Outreach Services," www.westervillepubliclibrary.org/outreach-services.
7. Brooklyn Public Library, "Outreach," www.bklynlibrary.org/outreach/older-adults/creative-aging.
8. Monica Anderson and Andrew Perrin, "Tech Options Climb among Older Adults," Pew Research Center, May 17, 2017, www.pewresearch.org/internet/wp-content/uploads/sites/9/2017/05/PI_2017.05.17_Older-Americans-Tech_FINAL.pdf.
9. Ohio Library Council, "Ohio's Public Libraries Improvise, Expand Service during COVID-19 Pandemic," http://olc.org/blog/2020/04/16/ohios-public-libraries-improvise-expand-services-during-covid-19-pandemic/.
10. Ally Dowds, "Boston Public Library Finds Ways to Safely Serve Homeless, Recovering Patrons Thru Pandemic," *Library Journal*, May 1, 2020, www.libraryjournal.com/?detailStory=boston-public-library-finds-ways-to-safely-serve-homeless-recovering-patrons-thru-pandemic.
11. Boulder Library Foundation, "Proud to Fund Innovative Library Programs That Bring Internet Connectivity to Those in Need during COVID-19," https://boulderlibraryfoundation.org/2020/06/01/proud-to-fund-innovative-library-programs-that-bring-internet-connectivity-to-those-in-need-during-covid-19/.
12. St. Louis County Library, "Book a Trainer," www.slcl.org/content/book-trainer.

NEVER LET A CRISIS GO TO WASTE

Removing Customer Barriers during COVID-19

— Cordelia Anderson —

The "marketing funnel" is a concept that describes how customers engage with your library, and then become repeat customers and eventually advocates. The marketing funnel applies to the library customer experience, and especially as library services are impacted by COVID-19, at a time when customers need us more than ever.

The marketing funnel concept describes the stages of a customer's relationship with an organization. They are as follows:

- Awareness
- Interest
- Consideration
- Evaluation
- Decision
- Action/Transaction
- Repeat
- Loyalty
- Advocacy

Picture a funnel, with the widest part at the top. That's the awareness stage. Imagine you can "pour" all your potential customers into the top of the funnel. As the funnel narrows, the person's relationship with your library strengthens, until they reach the action/transaction stage and become a customer. Examples of actions/transactions include a checkout, a website visit, attending a program, asking a reference question, making a donation, joining a Friends organization, or other interactions. From there, if they have a good experience, they become repeat customers and eventually move to the bottom of the funnel to become advocates.

Unfortunately, few libraries have designed their business models to move customers down the funnel. In fact, many libraries have done the opposite—we

FIGURE 14.1 | The marketing funnel.

have erected barriers inside of our funnels, making it difficult for customers to interact with us at every stage. As a result, customers leave, or escape from the funnel through "holes" that we ourselves have created.

These barriers can be even more of an impediment during the era of COVID-19. If libraries want to continue to grow and thrive, they need to fix the funnel. Here are three "holes" that should be your biggest priorities.

1 | LIBRARY CARD APPLICATION PROCESS

This impacts customers at the "decision" phase of the funnel. The library card sign-up experience is the first of many holes in the funnel. The sign-up process for most public libraries is clunky and slow. Many libraries still require a waiting period, and cards often have to be mailed to the customers, taking one or two weeks. Why? Because of policies and procedures that haven't changed with the times. Libraries exist to serve customers, so why don't we start thinking about how to engage customers as quickly and easily as possible?

When libraries had to close their doors due to the impact of COVID-19, some libraries lifted restrictions and expedited the process of issuing a library card so that customers could access digital resources without delay. My hope is that these libraries won't go back to "business as usual" when they reopen. These new processes provide an opportunity to do things differently and improve the sign-up experience.

How do we close the library card application hole in the funnel? Put the customer at the center of the conversation. Start by asking yourself, "What is the experience of getting a library card like for the customer?" Or better yet, ask your customers that question. Send a short survey to new cardholders. Their feedback can help you to improve their experience and increase customer conversion and retention.

2 | FINES AND FEES

This impacts customers at the "repeat" phase of the funnel. Your customer has moved further down the funnel. They have managed to get a card, have used it, and are ready to use it again. But wait! They can't. Why? They have a block on their account due to fines and fees.

Many libraries across the country have gone fine-free, and I hope more libraries follow suit. But many still use them. Fines and fees are some of the biggest impediments to customer retention; specifically, overdue fines. If you still charge overdue fines, ask yourself why. Depending on your library and who you ask, you may get different answers. Here are some examples:

- *To get people to return items and return them on time.* This is probably the most common reason and is probably why you started charging overdue fines in the first place. Most libraries that have gone fine-free have eliminated *overdue* fines, not fees for lost or damaged items.
- *As a revenue source.* Like it or not, many libraries have come to rely on fines and fees as a source of revenue. In some cases, these may be their biggest source of discretionary income. But ask yourself this: How much is this practice costing you? Collecting fines requires staff time. It disrupts customer interactions. Some customers simply give up and stop using the library. How much time, energy, and money do you spend trying to lure people into your library with programs, marketing campaigns, or new services? You are wasting that effort by simultaneously luring in and driving away people because of this practice. It's counterintuitive.

- *As a punishment.* Admit it. Sometimes we get frustrated with customers not returning items, and we want to penalize them. We say things like, "We give customers lots of chances. Why are we giving them more? They should just renew their items or return them on time." My response is that it's a better practice overall to keep customers engaged with the library. If customers don't or can't renew their items, maybe we aren't making it convenient enough for them. And more importantly, are we in the *punishment* business or the library business?

How do we close the fines and fees hole in the funnel? It may not be possible to eliminate fines and fees overnight, but you can take a look at other libraries that have done it successfully and begin laying the groundwork now. Look carefully at the number of people affected by fines, as well as the impact of collecting them on your internal operations and efficiency. Become educated about where your limits are and how you handle fine balances over a certain amount. Finally, put yourself in the customer's shoes. Don't start with all the reasons it would be hard to eliminate or reduce fines and fees. Start with the one compelling reason why it would be great to eliminate them: offering truly free and equal access to all.

3 | AUTO-EXPIRING CUSTOMER ACCOUNTS

This impacts customers at the "repeat" and "loyalty" phases of the funnel. Many public libraries have a process in place to "expire" library accounts after a set period. The logic behind this is that some library customers may have moved out of the community, and the library wishes to verify that these customers are still eligible for a library card. To un-expire the account, a customer must usually visit the library in person and show an ID or some other proof of residency. During the visit, the account is reactivated for a set period, until it auto-expires again.

The usual justification for this practice is twofold: (1) it prevents someone who no longer lives in the community from having a library card for which they are no longer eligible, and (2) it provides the library with updated account information for eligible customers.

However, this practice has many disadvantages that outweigh the benefits. First, it hurts the customer relationship. Even the most loyal library user may still find that their account has expired, and when this happens it doesn't make sense to them. In my library career, I have heard from several frequent library users who were upset when their accounts expired. For them, expiration is something that is only supposed to happen when you *don't* use your account, so having an active account expire seems illogical. Second, it adds yet another barrier for less frequent library users, online-only users, or users with access barriers. Many library customers simply don't have the time or transportation to visit a library in person when their account expires. This is especially true right now during the COVID-19 pandemic. Someone who is using e-books or other online resources may not visit a physical library but is still a frequent user. Expiration may be the last straw for that customer, causing them to stop using their account.

Perhaps the most alarming fact of all is that many libraries don't even notify their customers of this practice. The way it plays out is that a customer tries to use their account and it simply doesn't work. They have no idea why.

This practice hurts customers, from the most advantaged to the most disadvantaged.

It's important to take a step back from this practice and ask yourself this question: "What's the worst thing that might happen if we *don't* auto-expire accounts?" The answer might be that people who have moved out of the community will still use the library. Okay. So what? How many people is that: a few hundred? A few thousand? Regardless of your library's size, it's probably far fewer people than you might think.

Now ask yourself this: "What's the worst thing that will happen if we *do* keep auto-expiring accounts?" How many customers, people who still live in your community, will be impacted? How many will wonder why their account doesn't work, and then possibly give up? The number of legitimate customers who are negatively impacted by this practice far outnumbers the number of people who have moved away.

How do we close the auto-expiring hole in the funnel? Thankfully, many libraries have eliminated this practice since the start of the pandemic, and I strongly encourage these libraries to make this a permanent change. I also encourage those who haven't made this change to do so immediately. There are many creative ways to accomplish what you want without disrupting customers. Why not focus instead on having a campaign to gather accurate contact information about your customers? This would allow you to communicate with customers about their accounts, as well as about the programs and services that are available while your physical locations may be closed or provide only limited access. As you gather these e-mail addresses, review your existing account-related communications and see where there might be gaps. Are you telling customers what they can expect from their library accounts and when? How are you minimizing disruptions to their usage of the library?

IT'S TIME TO FIX THE FUNNEL

Libraries have an advantage over for-profit businesses because our services are free and there is much goodwill toward libraries out in the world. That has saved us from losing more customers from our marketing funnels. But it doesn't give us a pass. Think how much more we could do for our communities if we could remove these holes and barriers from our marketing funnels. Think how many more customers we could serve and help. Not to mention the increases we would see in library activities such as circulation, program attendance, and digital usage.

Making these kinds of bold changes is especially important now during the COVID-19 pandemic. This is a time when the needs of our communities and customers are even greater, while the funding that goes to libraries is threatened by economic challenges. There has never been a better time to fix your funnel.

HELPING STUDENTS SUCCEED DURING COVID-19

— Cindy Mediavilla —

ifty-five million students finished their studies from home in spring 2020, after 130,000 K–12 schools nationwide had closed their doors due to the coronavirus pandemic. Teachers struggled to adapt to an online environment, while parents scrambled to find child care. The situation was dire, prompting one school administrator to compare the new reality to "playing a game of 3-D chess while standing on one leg in the middle of a hurricane."[1] The anticipated learning outcomes for stay-at-home students were grim. "Missing school for a prolonged period will likely have major impacts on student achievement," education experts Megan Kuhfeld and Beth Tarasawa predicted.[2] "Once schools are back in session, we must be prepared to support students, many of whom will likely be behind academically." By the end of the school year, teachers estimated that only 6 in 10 students were regularly engaged in online learning. The barriers included unreliable internet connectivity, older children taking care of younger siblings, and the lack of familial educational support.

HOW CAN PUBLIC LIBRARIES HELP?

In late March 2020, the Public Library Association (PLA) conducted a weeklong survey asking how the health crisis had affected public library operations. Over 2,500 public library systems responded, representing nearly 30 percent of U.S. jurisdictions. Although closed to the public, libraries continued many critical activities, such as linking to online COVID-related resources, using makerspace equipment to generate medical supplies, and creating virtual exhibits and programs. Thirteen percent of libraries still loaned laptops and Wi-Fi hotspots, but only 7 percent claimed to offer services in support of distance learning (e.g., loaning materials, and providing digital resources and internet access).[3]

Connectivity

According to the Pew Research Center, the internet has been essential to 53 percent of U.S. adults during the pandemic.[4] And yet, as many as 42 million U.S. households don't have access to the internet, because they either have no broadband, don't own a computer, or can't afford to pay subscription fees.[5] "The inequity in access to technology and education has never been so obvious," one educator observed.[6] Indeed, 21 percent of homeschoolers and 36 percent of low-income families don't have access to a computer.[7]

To help mitigate this inequity, many public libraries are lending out Chromebooks and tablets, along with portable Wi-Fi hotspot devices, to students for the entire semester. In addition, 93 percent of the public libraries that responded to the PLA's survey reported that they now leave their Wi-Fi on while closed. Passwords are often either posted on a sign outside the library or are not required. In Pottsboro, Texas, the library installed a wireless access point on the building's roof to extend its "parking lot Wi-Fi." In Kansas, the Topeka and Shawnee County Library repurposed two of its bookmobiles as traveling Wi-Fi hotspots.[8] In Virginia, the Williamsburg Regional Library's website includes a map of free Wi-Fi hotspots located throughout the community (www.wrl.org/wrl-comes-to-you/wrl-wifi-hotspots/).

Online Resources

Libraries have long provided web links to educational sites that are targeted directly at students. In Oregon, the Multnomah County Library's online Homework Center (https://multcolib.org/homework-center) is an excellent example of a well-curated collection of school-related e-resources. Many libraries also offer one-on-one tutoring through Brainfuse or Tutor.com. But what about parents—and even teachers—who are tasked with developing virtual lessons? Among the best resources is Wake Forest University's free tutoring site, which includes links to educational art projects, STEM activities, grammar and history lessons, reading exercises, and more, all conveniently organized by grade level and student ability (https://communityengagement.wfu.edu/virtual-engagement/virtual-tutoring/).

Moreover, online reading tools can help prevent what educators are already calling "the COVID slide."[9] The San Diego County Library, for instance, has partnered with OverDrive to provide free e-books to students from five school districts. A Sora app allows OverDrive to automatically authenticate student borrowers using their school identification, so no library card is needed. Fiction and nonfiction e-books are available through OverDrive for student readers of all ages. Hoopla and California's Enki (enki.biblioboard.com) also make e-books available through public libraries.

Reaching Out to Schools

Students and their families were by no means the only people surprised by COVID-related school closures. "Frankly, we were all thrust into remote learning in the spring," charter school director Ian Holm admits. "And, you know, not everyone was ready for that."[10] To help educators provide the best teaching experience possible, the librarians who staff the Brooklyn Public Library's "Brooklyn Connections" program have continued to provide remote outreach to schools even during the pandemic (www.bklynlibrary.org/brooklyncollection/connections). The program includes online instruction on how to conduct research, and offers virtual office hours where students, teachers, and parents can get one-on-one help with their projects. "We meet the schools where they are," says educating librarian Jen Hoyer, who recently visited a class of fifth-graders. The teacher was so pleased that she asked Hoyer to repeat the virtual session for the students' parents, which she gladly did.

Kaitlin Holt, also at the Brooklyn Public Library, recommends creating an agenda of activities to guide a librarian's virtual class visit. Kaitlin always confers with the teacher first by asking: "How many students and which grade level will be watching? Which topic(s) is the class studying? Should the lesson be synchronous or asynchronous? Should it be recorded? And which video instruction platform is preferred?" Video presentations are best made in front of a plain background, and all text should be read aloud since not everyone can see, read, or process print information. The Brooklyn Library's virtual sessions usually last around thirty minutes.

Homeschoolers and Learning Pods

Public libraries have worked in "perfect partnership" with homeschooled families since the 1980s.[11] Libraries provide space and programs for home-schoolers and may even, as in Madison, Ohio, pull together book kits related to a particular lesson topic.[12] In Tennessee, the state library created a "libguide" of essential resources, including links to homeschool legal requirements (https://tsla.libguides.com/homeschoolingforlibraries). The Los Angeles Public Library's "Homeschooling Resources to the Rescue" page lists relevant web links and e-books for "new, unexpected homeschool parents" who are suddenly having to help their children with remote learning (https://lapl.org/collections-resources/blogs/lapl/home-school-rescue).

Homeschooling is now more prominent than ever as families join together to educate their children via "learning pods." A relatively new teaching phe-nomenon, these pods may resemble in-person or virtual homework centers where a trained educator or parent assumes responsibility for helping several students to complete their schoolwork. Learning pods may also take the form of an independent homeschool where a small group of children are taught either online or in person. Libraries usually reach out to these groups via Nextdoor or various "pandemic pod" Facebook pages.

SILVER LINING

The Afterschool Alliance urges educational institutions to view the current crisis as an opportunity to reconnect with community partners.[13] Library media specialist Ashley Cooksey concurs. When asked to consider the long-term implications of a post-coronavirus world, she envisions an opportunity for strengthening relationships between public libraries and schools. "I'm hopeful that this [can lead to] an advocacy tool for library collaboration," she says, "and that [schools] can also build . . . even stronger partnerships with public libraries."[14] Let's make this happen!

NOTES

1. Sarah Darville, "Reopening Schools Is Way Harder Than It Should Be," *New York Times,* July 23, 2020, www.nytimes.com/2020/07/23/sunday-review/reopening-schools-coronavirus.html.

2. Megan Kuhfeld, and Beth Tarasawa, "The COVID-19 Slide: What Summer Learning Loss Can Tell Us about the Potential Impact of School Closures on Student Academic Achievement," May 2020, Collaborative for Student Growth, nwea.org/content/uploads/2020/05/Collaborative-Brief-Covid-19-Slide-APR20.pdf.

3. https://bit.ly/2By36Yp.

4. Emily A. Vogels, Andrew Perrin, Lee Rainie, and Monica Anderson, 2020, "53% of Americans Say the Internet Has Been Essential during the COVID-19 Outbreak," April 30, 2020, Pew Research Center, www.pewresearch.org/internet/2020/04/30/53-of-americans-say-the-internet-has-been-essential-during-the-covid-19-outbreak/.

5. John Busby, Julia Tanberk, and BroadbandNow Team, "FCC Reports Broadband Unavailable to 21.3 Million Americans: BroadbandNow Study Indicates 42 Million Do Not Have Access," February 3, 2020, BroadbandNow, broadbandnow.com/research/fcc-underestimates-unserved-by-50-percent.

6. Cynthia García Coll, "My Turn: Cynthia García Coll: Let's Not Forget the Children during Pandemic," *Providence Journal*, June 3, 2020, providencejournal.com/news/20200603/my-turn-cynthia-garciacutea-coll-letrsquos-not-forget-children-during-pandemic.

7. Vogels et al., "53% of Americans," www.pewresearch.org/internet/2020/04/30/53-of-americans-say-the-internet-has-been-essential-during-the-covid-19-outbreak/.

8. James K. Wilcox, "Libraries and Schools Are Bridging the Digital Divide during the Coronavirus Pandemic," *Consumer Reports*, April 29, 2020, consumerreports.org/technology-telecommunications/libraries-and-schools-bridging-the-digital-divide-during-the-coronavirus-pandemic/.

9. Kuhfeld and Tarasawa, "The COVID-19 Slide," nwea.org/content/uploads/2020/05/Collaborative-Brief-Covid-19-Slide-APR20.pdf.

10. Anya Kamenetz, "Can Online Learning Be Better This Fall? These Educators Think So," NPR, July 28, 2020, www.npr.org/202/07/28/895720240/can-online-learning-be-better-this-fall-these-educators-think-so?utm_medium=RSS&utm_campaign=news.

11. Christyna Hunter, "The Perfect Partnership: Public Libraries and Homeschoolers," *Public Libraries Online,* April 9, 2014, publiclibrariesonline.org/2014/04/the-perfect-partnership-public-libraries-and-homeschoolers/.

12. Grace Hwang Lynch, "Homeschooling Families Tap into Library Services, From Storytime to Science Equipment," *School Library Journal*, March 10, 2020, www.slj.com/?detailStory=Homeschooling-Families-students-Tap-into-Library-Services-from-Storytime-to-Science-Equipment.

13. https://bit.ly/3clwqQi.

14. https://bit.ly/3iVIhXI.

PANIC, PIVOT, AND PRESS PLAY

Launching Virtual Services
for Businesses and Nonprofits

— Gillian Robbins and Caitlin Seifritz —

The Free Library of Philadelphia is the public library system for the city of Philadelphia. The Free Library closed its doors in March 2020, when COVID-19 struck. The library's closure stretched from weeks into months, and we only began reopening in August 2020 for limited in-person services. In the interim, our website became the central branch of the library, serving our communities through robust online resources and virtual services.

The Business Resource and Innovation Center (BRIC) is housed in the Free Library's main library, the Parkway Central building. The BRIC creates multiple entry points for those with ideas, plans, skills, and passions, enabling people to make fact-based business decisions in order to fulfill their goals. We assist entrepreneurs, nonprofits, job-seekers, and inventors at every stage, helping to improve their skills through public programs and appointment-based, individualized guidance in research and planning, and a curated collection of print and digital resources.

As part of the renovation of the Parkway Central Library, the Business Resource and Innovation Center opened a new, 8,000-square-foot space in April 2019, with flexible spaces for co-working, meetings, and programs. In the new space we served nearly 9,000 people, hosted 210 programs, and had 324 research appointments before closing in mid-March 2020.

These past months have been challenging, scary, and overwhelming, but the BRIC proved ready to meet the challenges. We have built well-rounded virtual services for Philadelphia's business and nonprofit community. We learned a lot along the way, and are excited to continue to support the community we serve.

VIRTUAL SERVICES

Immediately upon closure, the BRIC staff turned to virtual services. The core services became virtual programs, virtual research appointments with librarians, and a library of video content.

Programs

The BRIC's programming is broken into two categories: librarian-led classes and partner programs. The librarian-led classes on conducting research, such as market research or research on funding opportunities, were tweaked to reflect the current needs of virtual audiences. Breaks for questions were added more frequently, and classes were shortened to reflect the digital attention span. We also made the classes more interactive by using Zoom features such as breakout rooms and poll questions. Our partner programs focused on topics relevant to COVID-19 needs, such as loan programs and moving services online.

Appointments

Beginning in May, we transitioned our popular research appointments to a virtual format. By using a Google form (bit.ly/virtualbric1on1), business owners and nonprofit professionals can request a forty-minute session to learn how to use business and fundraising databases. The appointments are tailored to their specific needs and industry. Entrepreneurs can request assistance with general business planning, finding their target audience, creating a competitive analysis, and sales lists. As librarians, we cannot offer an in-depth analysis of business plans, but we use databases to help facilitate the research and explain the process. For example, a customer recently opened a small café and requested an appointment on the topic of market research. After speaking with her for a few minutes about her business, the librarian determined that she needed to define her target audience more before conducting market research, because she was casting her net too wide. Therefore, staff demonstrated market research and demographics databases while explaining the research processes, database functions, and next steps. To date, we have conducted nearly fifty virtual appointments via Zoom.

Video Content

People are working at unconventional times right now and cannot always attend a morning workshop—even a virtual one. So the BRIC staff use the record feature in Zoom to record programs to post on the Free Library's YouTube channel. All of the business programs are grouped together under "Business Resources" (bit.ly/bricbizdiglib). We add the latest classes to the playlist and promote them in our newsletters and on social media.

The video content is a helpful referral tool when a user needs assistance with a topic but cannot attend a live (online) program. In addition to recording live workshops, BRIC staff recorded short videos on accessing and using our databases and on the elements of a business plan. Pro tip: Write a script to ensure that you are succinct and professional.

Lessons Learned: Accessibility

Access to the internet has been a sticking point in our move to virtual services. In Philadelphia, over one-quarter of the population does not have access to the Internet at home.[1] While moving our services online was a benefit to many of our users, we understand that we are not reaching everyone. On the other hand, providing virtual services removes one barrier: physically getting to the library. Transportation, disabilities, child care, weather, and scheduling conflicts are among the reasons why users may be unable to come to the Business Resource and Innovation Center. Offering services virtually removed some of these barriers. Furthermore, offering recordings of our workshops and training videos allows people the flexibility to view content at their convenience, at any time of day.

THE POWER OF PARTNERSHIPS

One of the first things the BRIC staff did when the Free Library closed was talk to our partners. Before Zoom exhaustion set in, we held virtual meetings and exchanged e-mails with our closest partners, including local government agencies, other technical providers, and programming partners. It was important to understand what our partners were doing to support businesses and nonprofits in order to avoid the duplication of services. It also helped us better refer users and curate resources for the public. Additionally, collaborating with partners reminded us that we were all working together to serve the community.

The first order of business was to understand the scope of services still being provided by our partners to businesses and nonprofits during the closures. We reached out to our existing network of technical providers and to the city of Philadelphia's Commerce Department. While Commerce did its part to curate financial resources and programs, the BRIC took on the responsibility of working with technical providers to create an internal collaborative guide, with information on what each organization was providing virtually. This guide could be updated by organizations themselves to reflect rapidly changing information. The guide helped our staff quickly refer businesses to the proper resource or service. It also allowed for information to be disseminated on social media and during virtual appointments with a librarian. Finally, the guide provided contact information outside of traditional office phone numbers and general e-mail accounts.

Working closely with partner organizations helped the BRIC staff see the big picture so we didn't duplicate services already being offered elsewhere. For example, legal services were being offered by at least three other organizations, so the BRIC staff canceled our scheduled legal office hours and pivoted to accounting services, which were not offered elsewhere. Working with a local accounting firm that specializes in small business, we offer thirty-minute appointments with a CPA to discuss patrons' accounting needs and questions about taxes, payroll, and business structure, as well as COVID-specific questions.

The BRIC could not have maintained its programming without the help of its partner organizations. Many of them were willing to provide virtual programs. In March and April, our staff contacted organizations that were already scheduled to present a program to see if they would like to reschedule and present them virtually. The staff also reached out to our partners to support the new needs—which mostly involved emergency funding and were COVID-specific—of businesses and nonprofits. We relied heavily on our network of partners to refer and guide us.

Lessons Learned: Collaboration

The success of our virtual services could not have happened without the help and collaboration of our partners. We relied on partners to present programs and spread the word about our services, and we referred our users to their services when these were beyond our expertise or scope. We learned how valuable strong partnerships and collaboration can be when working toward a common goal.

COMMUNICATION AND PROMOTION

When the Free Library of Philadelphia shut its physical doors, we knew that our communication methods would have to change. Previously, we had relied heavily on foot traffic into the BRIC's new space, where we promoted co-working and offered services to get people in the door, like free headshots and coffee.

Before COVID-19 struck, the BRIC maintained robust newsletters and social media accounts. As the pandemic set in, we understood that these would be our main forms of communication with users. We provided targeted information on those of our services that were going virtual, and we curated lists of resources and partner services in our newsletters. To grow our mailing lists, during program registration, we asked if users would like to receive our newsletters.

We kept our information clear and let users know that we were not going anywhere, despite our physical closure. It was important to communicate that our reference and appointment-based services were still available remotely.

We also made sure to keep our social media accounts current, knowing that many people go to Twitter for their news. In addition, we kept close tabs on the Twitter accounts of our partners and governmental departments, and retweeted relevant news, resources, and events to our users.

BRIC staff members also contribute posts to the Free Library's blog to further promote our services, resources, and video content. Our blog series, *BRIC at Home*, shares news and information about databases and resources that can be accessed from home (https://libwww.freelibrary.org/blog/tag/business-resource-innovation-center). For example, two databases, Simply Analytics and Foundation Directory Online, were previously only accessible at the library. During the COVID-19 closure, however, vendors made versions of those databases available remotely and we promoted that information heavily in our newsletters, social media, and blog posts. The usage of Simply Analytics, a mapping and data visualization tool for demographics, has increased significantly now that it is available remotely. In March, when it was only available at the library, it had 55 hits that month. Since being made available remotely, it has averaged over 200 hits per month.

Lessons Learned: Resource-Sharing

Effective internal communication leads to better public service. You should keep your staff up-to-date on the library's services for businesses and nonprofits.

Resource-sharing is a huge aspect of librarianship, and it does not end with the user.

As an institution largely known for its physical presence, it is difficult to convey to the public how the library can be open while its doors are closed. We learned that having a large mailing list and strong social media presence prior to the pandemic helped us quickly and effectively share information about our switch to virtual services. We also learned to keep our communications short and targeted, since people were being inundated with newsletters and alerts. We wanted the BRIC to be a source of clarity, not an additional point of stress.

WHAT WE LEARNED

In July, we created and sent out surveys to our users asking for feedback about our programs and services. The survey included a section on the impact of COVID-19 and the use of the BRIC's virtual services. The responses gave us a better sense of what businesses and nonprofits were struggling with and what their top needs were.

Of particular interest was how users were engaging with our virtual services and whether or not they would continue to engage with the BRIC virtually. About 91 percent of respondents said they would prefer either virtual services or a combination of virtual and in-person services once the pandemic subsides.

Through the survey results and input from our staff and partners, we learned that users like flexibility in services. Learning is not one size fits all. Therefore, we plan to offer virtual services in tandem with in-person services when we return to full capacity. Giving people the option to choose the format that best suits their needs allows us to meet more people where they are.

NOTE

1. U.S. Census Bureau, "QuickFacts: Philadelphia County, Pennsylvania," www.census .gov/quickfacts/philadelphiacountypennsylvania.

EARLY LITERACY SERVICES DURING LIBRARY CLOSURES

— Rachel Payne and Jessica Ralli —

When the Brooklyn Public Library closed its branches in March 2020, there was an intense adjustment period as we realized we had to find a way to continue delivering early childhood services to Brooklyn families. Storytimes, our bread-and-butter programming, and the most impactful way to deliver resources, information on early literacy, parent support, and more, had to go virtual. Nearly six months into the pandemic, we have now reopened many of our locations for lobby service only, while our in-person programming and services remain virtual. We've learned a lot, adjusted many practices and expectations, and found that there are some silver linings in this new normal.

VIRTUAL STORYTIMES

The Brooklyn Public Library (BPL) was one of the first libraries to offer virtual storytimes when we had to suspend in-person programming and close our libraries. We were able to pivot quickly since we had staff ready to offer programming and a marketing team standing by to give support.

Virtual Storytimes on Facebook Live

We have found that offering our Virtual Storytimes on Facebook Live is a great way to connect and balance the dynamic performance aspect of storytimes with digital interactivity. By using the comments function, we can engage viewers when the program is live. Here are some strategies that have made our storytimes successful.

Virtual Storytime Monitors

At all of our Virtual Storytimes on Facebook Live we have found it essential to have a page administrator behind the scenes who is monitoring comments, engaging families, and offering troubleshooting assistance to the program leader. The monitor can also hide off-topic comments and ban users who are making inappropriate or abusive comments. Monitors can also share the program with the BPL's branch Facebook pages.

Diverse Storytime Presenters

Since virtual storytimes are quite public and can get shared far and wide, it is essential that our storytime leaders reflect the communities we serve. While children's librarianship is primarily white and female, making a conscious choice to have staff members and special guest readers of color, as well as male staff members, has been something we have worked hard to achieve. A group of children's librarians started an informal, biweekly Antiracist Storytime meet-up to share storytime tips for incorporating antiracist practices into our virtual programming.

Multilingual Programs

To date, we have offered Virtual Storytimes in approximately ten languages, and we discovered that these programs have been some of the best-received. Our Tibetan Storytime has been a viral hit, since we are lucky to have a Tibetan-speaking children's librarian. Her programs have been viewed more than 27,000 times across the globe. If we don't have Youth Services staff who speak a particular language, we look for other bilingual staff members or talented performers who can offer programs as contractors through grant funds. Many of our multilingual programs this past spring focused on the U.S. 2020 census as a means of spreading the word to linguistically diverse communities in Brooklyn.

Recorded Storytime Programs

Some of our staff members are uncomfortable presenting live. We have also had elected officials, donors, teen volunteers, and multilingual staff who want to be paired up with a children's librarians to offer storytimes. So we started making prerecorded storytimes that could then be shared on social media. We have found that recording a storytime on Zoom and then sharing the recorded program as a Facebook Premiere video works best. We find we get more views with Facebook, since that platform notifies more users than we do with YouTube. Another benefit of prerecorded programs is that Facebook and YouTube will caption the programs to make them more accessible.

Zoom Storytime Programs

While Facebook Live has made it relatively easy to create consistent and reliable storytime programs, Zoom has allowed us to transition some of our more

FIGURE 17.1 | A pride-themed virtual storytime with Kat.

interactive, intimate programs to the digital world as well. "Brainy Babies" is a BPL storytime and parent support program for children from birth to age three and their caregivers, supported by the FUEL Initiative of the Robin Hood Foundation. It is a neighborhood-specific program that focuses on connecting families to community resources and sharing brain-building and early literacy tips with parents and caregivers through interactive storytimes, with a focus on extended play and socialization. Our team transitioned this interactive, play-based program to Zoom a few weeks after our branches closed, and we retained many of the families who came to the live programs by reaching out to them via text messaging, e-mail, and our community partners. Here are some of the more successful elements and lessons we learned from the Brainy Babies program.

Build a Team

Sometimes it takes a village! Brainy Babies regularly hosts between 20 and 25 families, and since the goal is to engage each individual child and family, we found that a team ensures that engagement is happening in lots of different ways. Whether it's adding multilingual content, sharing songs and rhymes, or having someone on hand to make sure the technology is running smoothly, a team can help make a Zoom program more engaging for each individual participant.

Have a Plan

Know your roles! It helps to have a clear run of the show, or plan who will deliver what content and in what order. Be sure to have a backup plan if the technology fails one of your facilitators—having an extra book or song on hand can save the day.

Show and Tell

Plan at least one activity where the children, no matter how young, have a moment to shine and interact. In Brainy Babies, each child brings a favorite toy, stuffed animal, or costume to share at a designated time each week. Parents and facilitators help by asking open-ended questions to encourage the child's language development.

Virtual Outreach

While most of our tried-and-true strategies for in-person outreach are on hold, we've found that texting and e-mailing families helps keep them engaged and coming back. The Brainy Babies team creates weekly newsletters that share links for the next program, as well as neighborhood-specific resources, adorable photos of participants, and early literacy tips.

PARENT WORKSHOPS

Workshops for the parents of young children are a staple of our in-person early childhood services. In the virtual world, as parents were navigating new and unprecedented challenges raising and even schooling young children, we began to offer virtual parent workshops on topics that were increasingly relevant. As school begins, we'll begin to roll out more early literacy-focused workshops, but here are some of the more timely topics that we found were in high demand.

Screen Time Balance

Before COVID-19 struck, Kymberly Konty, our early literacy outreach associate, had already developed a workshop for parents and educators on young children and technology. In partnership with Common Sense Media, we were able to offer this program virtually in both Spanish and English. The parents learned about the American Academy of Pediatrics guidelines, best practices around joint-media engagement, and how to set healthy limits as a family.

Talking about Race for Parents and Caregivers

In the wake of recent police brutality and violence, and the many Black Lives Matter protests that followed, we found that parents and caregivers were looking for books to help spark conversations about racism with young children. In June we hosted the first in a series of workshops to help support this important dialogue in age-appropriate ways using books as conversation starters.

Ready Set Kindergarten

Normally held in person at 30 of our 60 branches, "Ready Set Kindergarten" is an enhanced storytime and parent workshop rolled into one. Held on weekends, it is a way for parents and children to learn together and get ready for school. We switched to a virtual format via Facebook Live, keeping the same facilitators, schedule, and curriculum. This fall we'll launch a Zoom version of the program, which will help parents who are guiding their children through remote learning by aligning their book and activities with pre-K and K curricula, and providing the parents with tips for learning at home.

PROFESSIONAL DEVELOPMENT FOR LIBRARY STAFF

Our library staff are also navigating a new world, and to keep everybody up to speed we wanted to provide them with innovative learning experiences.

Webinar Series

When we had substantial grant funding to use before the end of our fiscal year, we moved fast to schedule webinars on a range of early childhood topics that are of interest to children's librarians and other educators. We kept each webinar to one hour and tried to include a range of practical, bite-sized topics (e.g., using scarves as masks) and important and timely information (e.g., toxic stress and early brain development). Because we could have up to 100 people attend the sessions, we invited children's librarians from across New York state and educators from throughout Brooklyn. We were able to record the webinars so that the staff could participate asynchronously. We plan to continue offering the sessions this fall.

Virtual Storytime Meet-Ups

Since many staff members were struggling with virtual programming, we decided to offer weekly, one-hour meet-ups to discuss tips, best practices, and offer troubleshooting assistance. We usually have a short agenda and cover topics like hosting teen guest readers or how to make storytimes accessible, along with practical advice on how to use Facebook and Zoom. These sessions are very popular, with upwards of 60–70 staff members attending virtually.

Antiracist Storytime Meet-Ups

Inspired by a staff webinar led by Jessica Bratt, the youth services manager at the Grand Rapids (MI) Public Library, a group of children's specialists at the BPL decided to set up a bimonthly virtual meet-up to discuss ideas and tips for incorporating antiracist practices in our storytimes in age-appropriate ways. We have 35–45 librarians who attend regularly, and we've started planning and promoting virtual antiracist storytimes as a result.

SUPPORTING EDUCATORS

Despite the interruptions caused by the pandemic, we have continued to offer educational programming for educators.

Early Childhood Symposium

Our annual Early Childhood Symposium is normally an in-person meeting on an important topic for early childhood educators, but this year the symposium went virtual. The event, "Supporting Gender Diversity in Early Childhood Education," was open to educators, librarians, and other early childhood stakeholders. In prior years, some educators had difficulty attending the symposium due to scheduling conflicts, but this year we're all happy to be able to attend virtually. We even had educators outside of New York City join—an unexpected benefit of going virtual. We are now considering offering a portion of the in-person symposium in future years as a webinar, which will allow participants to attend both remotely and in person, improving its accessibility and reach.

Read with Me: Certificate in Early Literacy Practices for Caregivers

Piloted last year, this popular, four-session program is designed to share best practices in early literacy with nannies, caregivers, and other informal child care providers. At the end of the series, caregivers receive a Certificate in Early Literacy Practices from the library to use for their professional development and share with employers. We plan to launch a virtual version of the program in early fall of this year. This will not only allow us to reach a wider audience of caregivers, but also is an easier way to initially scale the program and train more librarians to be facilitators.

OUTREACH

Despite closures for both libraries and schools, library staff members continued our outreach efforts.

Virtual Class Visits

Even though many child care programs and early childhood programs have been closed due to the pandemic, some of our staff have found a way to continue to offer outreach to schools or child care programs. Here are some best practices for these virtual class visits:

- Let the school/program invite you to their online platform. If the school/program has a preferred platform and a scheduled meeting, you can be a special guest and share a read-aloud. Encourage the parents to join the class, if possible, so you can share information about library resources with them. Take some time to get to know whatever online platform the school/program is using.
- If the school doesn't have a digital platform, offer to set something up for them on your preferred platform. Make sure it is a relatively easy-to-use program so families can access it from home or teachers can access it in their classroom if they are back in session.
- Offer your Virtual Storytimes at a time you know they work for your local schools and child care programs. This is a great option if you have limited time during the week. Give the school a shout-out during the program if you know they'll be watching.

Texting Program

Many families don't have access to Facebook Live or Zoom, or they may have few digital devices at home. Our department decided that it made sense to invest in a text-messaging platform that would allow us to reach families via text, which is known to be more accessible to younger parents, immigrants, and low-income communities. We now have three texting programs that families can opt into (based on their children's ages) to receive one or two early literacy tips and activities per week, as well as information on upcoming virtual programming with direct links. Soon we will be adding Spanish. We plan to continue to use this valuable communication tool even after in-person programming resumes.

SILVER LININGS AND LESSONS LEARNED

While the shift to virtual programming has not necessarily been ideal for young children, there have been several silver linings and lessons learned. The response to our Virtual Storytimes has been tremendous. Families request their favorite librarians, and our programs have been viewed as far away as Australia and Zambia. There are some programs we plan on continuing virtually, since we know that coming to the library can be difficult due to disabilities, illness, weather, and busy work schedules. While our learning curve has been steep, we are pleased that many of our staff members are becoming more skilled at social media, video editing, and more. And this moment has allowed us to try new methods of outreach, such as texting, to reach people across Brooklyn.

TECH SUPPORT IN PUBLIC LIBRARIES DURING THE COVID-19 SHUTDOWN

— Luke Thompson —

Like many public libraries, the Evanston Public Library (EPL), located in the city of Evanston (pop. 74,000) on the northern border of Chicago, shut down in early March due to the COVID-19 pandemic. Evanston has a diverse population, perhaps most importantly with regard to wealth: its poverty rate is roughly 14 percent, with a median household income of about $60,000 in a city with a high cost of living. Due to these disparities, digital literacy, as well as access to physical hardware (e.g., computers) and paid online resources (databases, online courses, online exam preparation), differ considerably among Evanstonians.

Under normal conditions the EPL's digital resources and services include:

- 30 desktop computers for public use (including a computer designed for those with vision impairment)
- 20 additional computers in the Children's Department and the Teen Loft
- 200 hotspot devices that can be borrowed for four weeks at a time
- 3-D printers (in the Teen Loft)
- Scanners, fax machines, and photocopy machines
- Tech trainers who provide free, one-on-one private lessons six days a week, in English or Spanish
- Thursday tech tutorials: two 2-hour classes per week, each focused on a different topic
- E-books and audiobooks (Hoopla, Libby/OverDrive)
- Movie streaming (Kanopy)
- Access to online, subscription-based databases and websites (e.g., Ancestry, Morningstar)

- Mobile library: a minibus stocked with physical books, Chromebooks, and direct Wi-Fi access to library resources

ADAPTATIONS TO THE PANDEMIC

Upon our closure, we faced two immediate problems. First, many patrons were unaware of how to access our e-books, audiobooks, and movie-streaming service. In addition, they either didn't know about our other online resources, or they knew about them but didn't know that they could be used from home. We already had written instructions on how to use some of these services, but these instructions were not always clear or up-to-date. To remedy this, we immediately created a series of instructional videos that explained, for example, how to borrow and read a book from OverDrive using a web browser, the Libby app, or a Kindle; how to access the EPL's *Consumer Reports* account from home; and how to use Mango Languages, a language-learning service to which the EPL subscribes. We also forwarded the desk phones to library staff members' phones, so that patrons experiencing technical problems could call and get help. If the on-call staff member could not help the patron, then the patron was referred to one of our one-on-one tech trainers for further assistance.

The second immediate problem we faced was that we could no longer provide in-person tech instruction and support. Prior to the pandemic we offered two forms of instruction. First, we ran two 2-hour tech classes every Thursday, on topics ranging from how to use Word on an iPad to how to order groceries online. Second, we had about twenty 45-minute slots per week for one-on-one meetings with one of our tech trainers, meetings that could be conducted in English or Spanish. The content of these meetings was determined solely by the needs of the patron. In order to continue these two services, we moved both of them online. In the case of the Thursday tech classes, the move online actually increased attendance, from 10–15 to 25–30 attendees per meeting. This was probably due to the fact that these classes attract an older crowd, many of whom find it cumbersome to travel to the library for a class but can easily attend from the comfort of their own homes. This class also worked well as an online program because except for a short Q&A period at the end, the flow of information is one-way, from presenter to audience.

Moving the one-on-one sessions online, however, did not work as well. This was in part due to the difficulty of providing tech support and explanations over the phone to someone whose computer or device screen one cannot see.

Chapter 18

The decrease in use of this service might also have been due to the fact that many patrons sign up for the sessions only once they learn of their existence through conversations with library staff, conversations that were not happening because of the library's closure.

Due to the socioeconomic disparities in Evanston, there are many residents without computers at home or without internet access. Many of these people come to the library for all of their online needs, from writing e-mails to applying for jobs online, to printing out worksheets for their children. While we could not initially reproduce these services in full, library staff distributed hotspots and Chromebooks to many residents who lacked internet access or computers at home. In addition, the library, in partnership with the employment-assistance nonprofit National Able Network, is developing job-searching kits, which include tools job-seekers would need to access the internet from home, thereby allowing them to search and apply for jobs online.

Finally, in July, with restrictions easing, we opened a makeshift computer lab just inside the library's entrance in which we had a printer, scanner, and ten Chromebooks. Patrons had their temperatures taken prior to entering, had to wear masks, and were allowed to stay for no longer than an hour. We sanitized each computer after it was used. This lasted for three weeks, after which time the entire library reopened at a reduced capacity, our regular computer lab included.

OBSTACLES AND POSSIBLE SOLUTIONS

Providing tech support over the phone proved to be difficult. A problem that could be worked out in ten minutes in person turned into a frustrating, one-hour phone conversation. One solution I considered, but which I realized most libraries (including my own) would never sanction for a host of legal reasons, would be to view a patron's computer or device via a screen-sharing app (e.g., TeamViewer), thereby allowing the staff member to more accurately understand the patron's problem. Another possible solution (again, one that poses many legal hurdles) would be either to have a staff member provide roaming tech support, and the member would meet the patron in some outdoor location rather than have the patron come to the library; or to set up an area outside the library where patrons could bring their devices and receive in-person assistance.

In addition to the difficulty of providing tech support by phone, we faced the problem of not knowing precisely what services patrons did or did not need during the pandemic. Many of the tech issues with which I help people on a daily basis are not problems that patrons come to the library to solve, but are issues that are mentioned in the course of conversing with them and which I then address. Since the staff are not engaging in informal conversation with patrons during the pandemic, many of these issues are not mentioned and thus cannot be addressed. Wishing to tailor our services to patrons' needs, we began calling patrons who had made use of our one-on-one tech services during the previous few months and asked each person a list of questions about their digital needs, including whether they had internet access and computers in their home. While this did not result in a comprehensive data set for the entire population that we serve, it did give us a sense of what services we should maintain and which we might need to add.

ADVICE TO LIBRARIES GOING FORWARD

Looking back on my own library's experience, the advice I would give others trying to provide tech support and education during library closures would be to take the following actions, and in this order:

1. Move classes and programming online, but pay careful attention to which programs transfer well and which do not.
2. Assess your patrons' tech needs. These may be different during a pandemic than they are during times when the library is open. This can be done by calling patrons or by sending out surveys, and can be aided by a knowledge of the relevant statistics (e.g., the number of homes without internet access).
3. Be creative in thinking about how to provide services that cannot be moved online, and use the data collected in step no. 2 to create new services to meet new, pandemic-specific needs.

While the halt to in-person services was a shock to all of us, by following these steps libraries can not only continue to provide valuable services to patrons during closures, they will also be more innovative in delivering such services once they can reopen at full capacity.

MOVING BOOK CLUBS
AND READER'S ADVISORY ONLINE

— Becca Boland —

If you are like us at the Skokie (IL) Public Library, you probably went from being in the library talking about COVID-19 face-to-face to sitting in your home trying to figure out how you're going to interact with patrons when the library is closed. What worked for us is to take the things that we already did well and transfer them online.

ONLINE BOOK CLUB

At the Skokie Public Library, the first thing we put into motion was a way to make book discussions happen virtually. We started by selecting titles from an existing digital resource, Hoopla, because it allows our patrons simultaneous access to its materials. Hoopla has the Book Club Hub, and we used the books that are highlighted in that collection because they are available in both e-book and audiobook formats. We pulled out a handful of potential titles that we thought would appeal to both staff and our patrons.

When it came to choosing an online platform for our discussions, we discussed the pros and cons of Goodreads vs. Zoom at length and decided that we would use Zoom to host established discussions, but opt for Goodreads for a group of people who have never met or have no standing relationships with each other.

As a group, we established a list of book club guidelines so there was a reference if we needed to shift the discussion, but also to make sure that everyone knew they were welcome and their voices would be heard. (See the text box.)

Book Club Guidelines

- There is no one way to experience or interpret a book. In fact, we love it when people have different opinions about books (it makes for a better discussion). But please be gracious and respectful of each other's opinions. In other words, you can disagree but don't be disagreeable.
- Speak from your own experience using "I" statements. Refrain from generalizing based on a person's race, ethnicity, gender, religion, or socioeconomic class.
- Haven't finished the book yet? Join us anyway—you still have valuable insight. But please be aware that there may be spoilers in the club's discussion.

We hosted our initial book club discussion on Goodreads (www.goodreads .com/group/show/1071304-skokie-public-library). Initially, each book was divided into three parts for discussion, and we put all of our discussion questions in one discussion thread. After our first session, we realized that we needed to change this approach because of the way that Goodreads discussions are formatted. It is very hard to follow different questions in the same thread. It was more conducive to divide the questions into individual topics, instead of having one thread for the entirety of the discussion.

The Evolution of the Book Club

Meeting weekly to discuss just a portion of the book quickly felt overwhelming. We transitioned to meeting once per month and per book. The slower pace allows us to do more planning, and it feels far less frantic.

We generally develop 6–8 questions per discussion. One of them is always "Is there anything you wanted to discuss that we missed?" This question leads to some of our most interesting discussions.

We also added an Instagram live discussion to allow for even more passive participation (www.instagram.com/skokielibrary/). People don't need to have read the book to attend, and we can interact with patrons as they comment. This format is far more casual and often far sillier than a classic discussion, but it is regularly informed by the discussion that happened on Goodreads the week prior. The live discussions are saved to our Instagram feed, and people can watch them whenever it is convenient.

We've also expanded the titles beyond Hoopla to include the OverDrive/Libby cost per circ titles. This increases the options that we have for discussions, and it allows us more control over which titles we use.

In June, we chose *Here for It* by R. Eric Thomas. We were fortunate to have Thomas join us on Instagram. I interviewed him using questions developed by the book discussion team and by our patrons, who had participated in the Goodreads discussion.

We wrapped up summer reading with an open, hybrid book talk/book discussion on Zoom about what we had read over the summer—the good, bad, and in-between. At the end of the year, we will focus our monthly discussion on Staff Picks/Best Books of the year instead of choosing a specific title. We are also going to add Facebook Live (in addition to Instagram) in order to cover all of our social media bases.

We will continue to change and evolve as we host future book discussions online.

BOOKMATCH

It was also important to us to continue to have reader's advisory interactions that replicated the experience of asking for recommendations in the library. We didn't have to look any further than Bookmatch, a service that the Skokie Public Library has been offering for more than ten years (https://skokielibrary.info/books-movies-more/bookmatch/). In the Bookmatch service, there is a form embedded on our website that patrons can fill out with their reading preferences. They submit this form to us, and then we collaborate to create a customized reading list in BiblioCommons that we send out to each patron, which they can easily access through our website. (In addition to Bookmatch, we also have a Screenmatch service, which gives recommendations for films and TV shows.)

While not every library has the ability or opportunity to embed a form in its own website that readers can fill out, there are other options. At the Ela Area Public Library (north of Chicago), the Bookmatch service uses a Google form that has been embedded. Readers' responses on the form are automatically added to a spreadsheet, and an e-mail goes to a designated staff member. That staff member sends the spreadsheet out to other staff members who come up with a list of recommended titles for each reader, based on the preferences they expressed on the Google form. Then the staff member sends an e-mail to the patron that includes the list of recommended titles, with hyperlinks to the library's catalog.

The same information is provided by readers on the forms submitted to both libraries. They are just presented on two different platforms. And you don't even need to embed the form in your library's website. Just link the URL to the form wherever you get the most traffic—newsletter, social media, or wherever. You can also use paper forms, and provide them to patrons during curbside pickup or at the self-checkout, if that's what works for your library and your staff.

#Minimatch

For those people who don't want to wait a week (or two) for us to create their customized reading list, we have been offering #MiniBookmatch and #MiniScreenmatch on our social media accounts a couple times each month (https://twitter.com/skokielibrary). In these services, people can post their reading preferences on our Instagram and Twitter accounts, or else they can send a direct message to us on designated #Minimatch days, and our staff will collaborate on a short list of recommendations for them while they wait. In the actual transaction, our communications coordinator interacts with the patrons, allows us time to create a short list, and then shares the recommendations via social media. A related service, #MiniScreenmatch, works the same way, but offers while-you-wait recommendations for movies and TV shows instead of books.

BOOK CHAT

The SPL's Learning Experiences Department created a YouTube page specifically for programming while we are out of the building and can't have direct contact with our patrons (www.youtube.com/channel/UCwzDADYru1knA0HR7HI72xA/featured). The reader's advisory team started Book Chat, a program featured on that channel, as an opportunity to booktalk to our patrons. Every other week, we record staff members talking about books they have read, are reading, or are excited to read and want to share. Each booktalk is only one or two

---

Tips for Pandemic-Proof Book Lists

- Make book lists that focus exclusively on digital content, so people can access the materials without coming into the library.
- Make a list of books involving things that people want to be doing right now but can't (because of the pandemic), such as a collection of travel-focused books or films, or a list where every book has scenes that take place in a restaurant, at a sporting event, or at an amusement park.
- Create lists of short stories, or of books that are less than 200 pages long—these are quick and easy to read and seem obtainable. Readers don't need to make a huge time commitment to them, and they feel a great sense of accomplishment when they've finished.
- Create a list of fantastic audiobooks that patrons can listen to while they take a walk.

---

minutes long, at most. We include a full transcript for closed captions, as well as links to the materials we discuss in the notes. The videos are also posted to our library's Instagram page. This is an easily accessible and digestible asynchronous programming approach.

EVERYTHING YOU ARE GOOD AT, JUST ONLINE

Take a minute. Think about what you're really good at (not just now, but always) and move it online. Think about what resources you have available, and how you can adapt those services to work for you and your patrons right now. And remember, this is not a competition. It's a collaboration. Do you see something online that another library is doing really well? Use it. Do you see something really fun or cute on an indie bookstore's Instagram page or in an article you read that you would be willing to try? Do it. Reach out to other libraries if you have questions about how they did something. Don't reinvent the wheel. Be kind to yourself. You've got this.

THE CONNECTING POWER OF SOCIAL MEDIA

—Tiffany Breyne —

The year 2020 has not turned out the way any of us expected. Many libraries had big plans for this year, and they all got wiped away as the pandemic hit. One day my library canceled all in-person programs, and the next day we closed our building to prevent the spread of COVID-19. Things changed at a rapid pace, so we didn't have time to map out how to take our in-person services online, and we've been learning as we go ever since.

Here at the Skokie (IL) Public Library, we started a robust calendar of online events and found new ways to offer our services online. Social media has been essential in letting our patrons know that our librarians are still here for them. Here are a few ways we have used social media to compensate for the in-person engagement our patrons have been missing.

READER'S ADVISORY ON SOCIAL MEDIA

It is possible (and fun!) to transfer your reader's advisory skills to social media. The Skokie Public Library offers a service called Bookmatch (skokielibrary .info/bookmatch), wherein patrons fill out an online form that describes their reading preferences, submit the request via our website, and librarians create a customized list of recommended titles for the patron. It takes one or two weeks to provide the list to the patron. The library also offers Bookmatch for Kids and Screenmatch, which provides suggestions for television and movies.

We started doing #MiniBookmatch and #MiniScreenmatch on Instagram, Twitter, and Facebook. These services provide a list of recommended titles for each patron on a while-you-wait basis. Each service runs from 9:00 a.m. to 5:00 p.m. on a predetermined day once each month.

For #MiniBookmatch, we ask participants on each platform to give us information about their reading preferences, and then multiple librarians give recommendations based on those. Once we have about ten recommended titles, we send them to the participant, noting the name of the librarian who recommended each one. Our standard turnaround time is about forty-five minutes.

Adding the librarian's name for each recommendation is crucial because it allows the participant to know that our librarians are working to find a book just for them. And someday down the line, that person may come to the building, see a name tag, and recognize that staff member as the person who recommended a book they love. (Visit bit.ly/BookmatchIG to see a #MiniBookmatch session on Instagram.)

We have provided more than 300 book, movie, and TV show recommendations so far through these #Mini sessions, and several participants have reached out to thank individual librarians for their suggestions.

Tips for Implementation

- Offer reader's advisory on social media in a way that suits your library. The #Mini format works great for our team because they are already working online during the day, and having multiple people providing recommendations means that the work is done quickly and is diverse.
- Sometimes when we do these #Mini sessions, we don't have any participants, while at other times we have lots of them. Patrons' participation depends on many different external factors, so if you don't have any takers on some weeks, just keep at it.
- The #Mini format is a great option for staff members who prefer to work behind the scenes.

CONNECTING THE COMMUNITY WITH LIBRARY STAFF MEMBERS

People miss going to the library because of our essential services, but they also miss seeing and chatting with library staff. We have worked to keep that connection on our social platforms.

Instagram Stories

We use Instagram Stories (instagram.com/skokielibrary) to communicate useful information to our patrons. However, in order to add a personal touch, we had staff members provide reminders about the U.S. 2020 census, as well as a series of stories that offered tips on how to help others in our community, and other stories that celebrated National Bookmobile Day.

For the census Instagram stories, we chose a handful of topics to cover, including how the census impacts the community, the timeline for filling out the census, and whether a citizenship question is included on it. The staff prerecorded quick video snippets with this information. The final result was a series of Instagram stories; one story, with just text, would ask a question such as "Why should you fill out the #2020Census?" and this was followed by a video of a staff member answering the question. The next story after each video would have a text recap of what was said in the video, for followers who watch Instagram Stories with the sound off. This series has been seen nearly 4,500 times.

For National Bookmobile Day, our bookmobile team provided photos and videos detailing things they loved or missed about the bookmobile (since the service was not provided at the time). These were used in a series of Instagram stories, along with older Instagram posts showing the history of the bookmobile. The bookmobile is a beloved part of our library, so this series was popular with our followers, and it really worked because staff members added their personalities to it.

Summer Reading on Social Media

Like most libraries, summer reading was very different for us this year. We didn't track reading metrics as we usually do, and instead we created an Idea Book filled with six themes that people could follow in order to participate in summer reading. The themes were Read, Wander, Make, Share, Play, and Eat. The Idea Book was mailed to all households in Skokie with our bimonthly newsletter and then families could follow the ideas, such as listening to an audiobook, drawing a map of where they live, or inventing a new game to play. People e-mailed photos of the activities they did or tagged us on social media, and we created a Facebook album with their submissions.

FIGURE 20.1 | Summer reading at the Skokie Public Library.

At the beginning of summer, we scheduled social posts that emphasized the staff's participation in each summer reading theme. For our "Read" theme, we shared staff photos with or of books they planned to read this summer (bit.ly/SkokieReadFB). We continued to post more photos throughout the summer, since our followers liked to see what we were reading.

If staff members wanted to take part but didn't want to or couldn't take photos, we still shared their text submissions in conjunction with book covers or designs made using Canva.com. Visit bit.ly/SkokieTwitterRead for an example of this on Twitter, and bit.ly/SkokieIGRead for an example on Instagram.

Tips for Implementation

- When asking for staff involvement in social media, offer them options to accommodate their various levels of comfort. The photos that are posted can be of or by a staff member, or even of a pet. Sometimes staffers prefer to send only text, and you need to find a way to include imagery with it. That's okay. Be prepared to meet staffers where they are if you want mass participation.

- If you have staff members who love submitting content, that's great! Consider soliciting regular posts from these people, so that followers have something to look forward to.

- Getting staff members to take part in social media content can be difficult. Give yourself plenty of time, assign specific tasks to people, or create an editorial calendar—whatever helps you stay organized.

EXPLORING NEW PLATFORMS

With life's regularities thrown out the window during the pandemic, we've taken the time to explore new digital platforms and ideas.

Spotify

One online platform we ventured into was Spotify; we started a public Spotify account with music playlists curated by our staff members (bit.ly/SkokieS-potify). Because of the collaborative nature of our playlists, setting them up takes very little time, but the playlists give followers fun insight into our staff's musical tastes. If someone has an idea for a playlist, we create a Google Sheet where any staff member can add a song/artist, and then we create the playlist using the library's Spotify account. This is also great "evergreen" content that can be promoted during slow weeks.

Goodreads and Instagram Live

We also started an online book club. This club is open to everyone (not just Skokie residents), and we focus on one book each month. We then have two book discussions—one on Goodreads (bit.ly/SkokieGoodreads) and one on Instagram Live (bit.ly/SkokieIGLive).

On Goodreads, our staff moderates the discussion at a specific time and date, but members are welcome to add their thoughts at any time. On Instagram Live, the discussion is between two librarians having a spoiler-free and light-hearted conversation about the book. Viewers are welcome to comment or ask questions. Our Goodreads group has about 60 members, and our Instagram

Live discussions have anywhere from 50 to 150 live viewers. The goal for both platforms is that people decide their own level of participation. We realize that life is hectic and we can all handle only so many Zoom meetings, so these discussions are a way for our followers to engage with us with as much or as little effort as they would like.

Tips for Implementation

- If you're chatting about books, music, or movies, find the works' creators on each platform and tag them! We were able to host an Instagram Live discussion with the author of *Here for It; or, How to Save Your Soul in America* after tagging him on social media and starting a conversation with him. We have had other authors offer to do events with us as well, after we tagged them on social media.
- Start a Spotify account for your library now! It is low-maintenance, free, and a fun way for staff to show their personality.

Closing our building to prevent the spread of COVID-19 was necessary but heartbreaking. Despite that, our library and libraries across the country have found ways to still be there for our patrons. Keep up the tough work, creativity, and positivity—your patrons need it!

CONTINUING CULTURAL INCLUSIVITY PROGRAMMING DURING COVID-19

— Nicanor Diaz, Virginia Vassar Aggrey, and Naghem Swade —

T he Denver Public Library's Cultural Inclusivity Department is tasked with developing programs that help connect with our immigrant community. The department's mission is "collaborating with Denver's multicultural community to create equitable opportunities for learning, discovery, and connection." This is done through the Plaza program and intentional multicultural programming. The department consists of six staff members, including a program manager, program administrators, and librarians.

PLAZA PROGRAMMING

In early March—before the pandemic struck—a Tuesday evening at the Rodolfo "Corky" Gonzales Branch Library would be bustling with activity, the smell of coffee brewing, and the murmurs of many voices. Some people practice English together, while others work on homework assignments nearby, or drill civics flashcards to prepare for their U.S. citizenship exam. This was Plaza— weekly programming designed to build community and to make immigrant and refugee newcomers feel welcome at the Denver Public Library.

The library has been providing the Plaza program for over a decade. It began as a program aimed to help Spanish speakers connect with the resources they needed to thrive. Over the years, the program has expanded to be more inclusive, and now represents over fifteen languages spoken in the city of Denver.

Before COVID-19, eleven Plaza locations provided 48 hours of programming each week: English conversation tables, naturalization support, immigration legal help, job search assistance, and computer help, as well as activities for kids that allowed families to work and play in the same space. The Plaza program served approximately 25,000 participants a year. People from different parts of the world engaged with each other, learning things and building relationships. But overnight, the entire program shut down due to the pandemic. Knowing the importance of this programming, and the community it cultivated, Plaza's forty staff members pivoted quickly and learned to facilitate online. Within six weeks, the staff were leading six online conversation tables each week, as well as a citizenship study group and appointment services.

PROGRAMMING DURING COVID-19—OPPORTUNITIES

COVID-19 has created many new barriers, but as some obstacles sprang up, others were suddenly gone. Some participants in the now-online groups could never have made it to a library because of prohibitively long bus journeys or unforgiving work schedules. Many older adults faced health concerns or mobility issues that prevented their attendance. Suddenly, these customers are able to participate from the comfort and safety of their homes. Online groups are also attractive for those who are shy or introverted. There have been a surprising number of new faces participating in the Plaza program during the last four months. The staff have also found creative ways to facilitate engaging conversations online. Adult education lead Kalid Al-Rajhi, for example, has taken his group on virtual museum tours. Together, they have explored the Louvre and the Smithsonian Museum of Natural History in New York City, zooming in to read plaques and discuss what they observed.

Unlike dealing with transportation issues, the frustration of tackling new online tools can pay off in the development of tech skills. The staff have helped customers use their digital devices for new purposes, and now, when a new participant joins a group, other students often step in, or friends and family help each other get connected. Each time it gets a little easier. The training around resources helps the staff connect the program's participants with other organizations in the Denver area. As the quarantine began, the Denver Public Library worked with organizations across Denver to create and maintain a list of service interruptions caused by COVID-19, a list that is now used by more than 1,200 immigrant and refugee service providers in the metro area.

Online Challenges

Despite the connections these groups have created, our staff are still aware that for every one person connected, many more are left isolated and alone, without computers, internet access, or the tech skills needed to join an online class. To fill the gaps, our staff improvised a new appointment system to connect with people on a weekly basis. These connections happen mostly over the phone, to help with English, citizenship, technology access, unemployment insurance, and so much more. "It's a big challenge to start from square one by phone with a new English-speaker," says Amy Van Vranken, who hosts weekly calls with a newly settled refugee. Every Plaza staff member speaks at least two languages, so Amy is able to use French to aid in her communication. "Being able to have class by phone has filled a tech gap for a customer who doesn't have a computer. I'm grateful for his patience and determination!" The leader of citizenship programs, Amanda Savasky, described what she has learned about online teaching: "There are fewer social cues—facial and body cues—to guide the flow of conversation." Our staff have learned how much work it can take to create a natural feeling of spontaneity online or over the phone, but they remain committed to providing this access for immigrant and refugee customers.

CULTURAL INCLUSIVITY PROGRAMMING

Naghem Swade is the cultural inclusivity services coordinator for the Denver Public Library. She collaborates with multiple community organizations and partners to create and implement mindful programs that serve Denver's multicultural communities. Programs such as Lunar New Year, Stories of Light, Día del Niño/Día del Libro, and Día de los Muertos aim to establish trusting and authentic relationships with underrepresented community members. Transitioning to virtual programming has been challenging. Virtual spaces are not always equitable, nor are they accessible due to technological and other barriers. Another challenge of virtual programming has been engaging with the audiences that would benefit from these programs. Traditional public library engagement with immigrant and refugee communities has been mostly through English acquisition programs and naturalization efforts. Our aim is to create a foundation where library spaces can cater to the individual and collective needs of community members without enforcing our personal biases and assumptions of what some of those members might need. Our initial efforts were focused on transitioning the Plaza program virtually, while continuing to explore how to provide multicultural programming to intended community members. Moving forward, Naghem is focusing on the Stories of Light program series. These programs, a form of storytelling through dance, will focus on a global narrative. Seven stories from around the world will be highlighted to celebrate human joy and resilience.

OUTREACH DURING COVID-19

After a couple of months of virtual programming, some Plaza staff members began doing outreach at an apartment complex that houses immigrants. During these events, the staff connect with community members about their needs, provide free books, promote virtual events, and support the residents with tech access. Patrons are able to access the internet through a number of Chromebooks with hotspots provided by the library, and perform vital tasks like registering their children for school. One of the challenges for outreach during this time was developing guidelines that would ensure the safety of both staff and visitors while still connecting with the community. Our Mobile Services Department had developed COVID-19 health and safety guidelines for outreach and had been in the field early in April, and this was a great opportunity for us to team up with them to bring some resources to the apartment complex. The health and safety guidelines include using masks at all times, sanitizing and bagging books, maintaining six feet of distance with customers, and displaying books rather than handing them to patrons.

Since the start of the pandemic, library staff members have expressed the need to connect with Plaza program participants in person. This certainly has been one of the biggest challenges we have faced during the pandemic. As of this writing (September 2020), the staff are doing outreach at two locations on a weekly basis, and while this doesn't reach the large number of people we reached before COVID-19, it is still a step in the right direction. The staff continue to evaluate and pursue other outreach opportunities in collaboration with our Mobile Services Department.

SUPPORTING THE STAFF

While the Denver Public Library figured out how to better serve its customers during the pandemic, we quickly learned that our staff also faced technical challenges of their own. Staff members who didn't have access to the internet at home were able to borrow hotspots and Chromebooks so they could work from home. The staff began taking advantage of new training modules designed for virtual programming, while the library also began working on its policies for virtual programming. These policies were developed to help address concerns the staff had about confidentiality, accessibility, and privacy, particularly regarding Zoom and its vulnerabilities. Another concern addressed in the guidelines involved which online platform to use for virtual programs. Each digital platform comes with its own pros and cons, and we needed to make sure we were using the one that best fit the needs of our participants and staff. For example, Google Meet is the better tool when doing a program that relies on small group discussions. For large group discussions, Zoom is the better tool.

The last four months have certainly been challenging, but they have also taught our staff to slow down, take one task at a time, and be patient with one another. In doing so, the staff have developed new relationships and forged deeper connections with and between customers. After all, through shared challenges, empathy grows. Even with freezing screens, audio glitches, and faulty microphones, a moment of connection is a truly worthwhile endeavor. You can see what the Denver Public Library is currently offering for immigrants, refugees, and underserved populations by visiting www.denverlibrary.org/plaza.

WALK THIS WAY

Service Design for Clarity in a Disaster

— Jeffrey T. Davis —

The United States' handling of the COVID-19 pandemic has been a brutal and tragic disaster. The resulting loss of life, long-term disability, educational dislocation, impoverishment, stress, isolation, and trauma have been staggering. Compounding this, the harm has been grossly uneven, afflicting most grievously our most vulnerable populations and exacerbating our nation's serious inequities and injustices.

The rapid, collective suspension of inessential services that began in mid-March was squandered. Despite outpourings of grassroots mutual aid, month after month passed with unsteady messages and actions from the federal government and other seats of power. Responsibility for all this starts at the top, of course, and also owes to the long-running weakening of our social fabric and our economic reserves. Maddeningly, though, there were mistakes and failures by elites at every level—mistakes of communication, of analysis, of policy, and of operational response, layering damage upon damage. The efforts of states, counties, cities, the mass media, corporations, and institutions like the World Health Organization, the Centers for Disease Control, and the Food and Drug Administration, though well-intentioned, often contributed to the breakdown.

A crisis like the pandemic presents libraries' culture with a challenge. We have a deep bias in favor of authoritative sources of information. We teach this bias to students, we practice it with the public, and we defer to it to guide our operations. And most of the time, it's the right trade-off. While factual corroboration moves slowly and prerogatives compete, the true facts are relayed in the long run. What happens, then, when the government's official expertise is visibly steps behind the scientific community? And if that information is urgent, with vital individual and civic implications?

The COVID-19 pandemic has already seen several examples of this misguidance in the United States. In February and March 2020, the Centers for Disease Control (CDC) told the public not to wear masks, something we now know had tragic consequences. The county health departments that most libraries take their lead from generally repeated that guidance. The CDC corrected its position on April 3, well after evidence for the efficacy of masks in reducing transmission of the COVID-19 virus was clear and widely agreed on. The same pattern was repeated with regard to aerosol transmission of the COVID-19 virus, with big implications for library operations. The pattern repeated again with the matching of different types of COVID diagnostic tests to their appropriate use-case; with the directional emphasis of contact tracing; and with the prophylactic contribution of quiet. Because viral prevalence grows exponentially, these delays have compounded for an outsized impact on the population.

This is a novel virus and we have been learning and correcting our efforts continuously, so the point of reviewing these lags isn't to ascribe blame. To varying degrees they were inevitable, unremarkable, or have roots elsewhere. But they're tremendously consequential. A plurality of scientific researchers was again and again ahead of the government's official guidance. Libraries can't be satisfied to lag behind the best available understanding when designing their services during this pandemic. When we know better, it's not sufficient to demur to the authorities and defer our independence and responsibility.

INTO THE GREAT WIDE OPEN

The divide between indoor and outdoor transmission risks emerged early in the pandemic. Contact tracing in East Asia made it clear that transmission events almost always occurred indoors and centered on talking or eating. Outdoor transmission events were virtually absent from the record. We learned more about the primacy of aerosol transmission when basic behavioral changes are present, the tertiary role of fomite transmission, and the best mitigation measures as research went on. This should have been a clear signpost for libraries: indoor gatherings are high-risk and difficult to mitigate, while outdoor gatherings are low-risk and easy to mitigate.

This is relevant not just for how we adapt our library operations, but also for how we contribute to the public's perceptions of the crisis. The indoor/

outdoor divide has been communicated poorly or worse in most places. For example, news stories on case growth and indoor spreading events were routinely illustrated with images of (low-risk) beaches. Parks were closed while indoor gatherings were open. This unmistakably sent the wrong message. The creation, promotion, and modeling of low-risk, positive alternatives help everyone to avoid high-risk activities. It's a key ingredient in compliance and community well-being to say "these are the things we can safely do!" Libraries have a vital role in making this clear.[1]

It's well understood that public health is partly about education and communication. Clear, accurate, culturally sensitive, empathetic, and nimble messaging is needed for populations to respond to threats to their health. In a public health crisis, the quality of libraries' communication with their communities is part of the same effort. Our service design during COVID-19 contributes to community norms both for the public and for library staff. So we should not simply ask, "Is our service design safe?" but "Does it faithfully clarify what is low- and high-risk in general?"

The service designs of libraries in this pandemic have run the gamut: from masked indoor service to limited hours, to curbside pickup, to Chromebook patios, to fully remote service, with and without a surfeit of surface cleanings, and with many variations, permutations, and combinations. None of these are ideal for service delivery. Patio (and ad hoc patio) weather is unforgiving in some places and times.[2] Remote service is not an answer for all community members because of internet access barriers and the social media platforms that libraries often depend on. And indoors is hard to make low-risk without stripping away most activities.

Though constrained, outdoor services meet key objectives. They're low-risk, accessible, and—crucially, when paired with indoor closure—embody a clear message. Most often these outdoor solutions have taken the form of curbside pickup services. Other important outdoor services and programs were already in place but became special areas of focus. Many libraries safely adapted existing programs for the outdoors: leading outdoor crafts and storytimes, outdoor bingo, walking groups, gardening, insect exploration, and stargazing. All of which, if masked and relatively hushed, are both very low-risk and provide a necessary outlet for social gathering, learning, and camaraderie.

Other examples of low-risk programs include:
- *Storywalks, treasure hunts, urban hikes, and self-guided social history tours.* We don't have comprehensive information yet, but tracking done

by the Let's Move in Libraries initiative suggests that public libraries added over a hundred different types of these programs in the first four months of the pandemic.

- *Ticketed passes.* Many of the traditional offerings (museums, performances) of ticketed pass programs are closed, but libraries are providing their communities access to outdoor attractions like the CuriOdyssey outdoor science and nature center, the Fairytale Town outdoor children's museum, and botanical gardens like the Filoli Center, Ruth Bancroft Garden, and Hidden Villa farm and wilderness area. There is the potential for more passes along these lines, like state parks, zoos, kayak rentals, and more.
- *Portable social services.* Student lunch programs and health fairs took to outdoor delivery sites.
- *Curbside pickup services.* These have been widely implemented and are covered well elsewhere. I'd only add that these services may have given too little attention to the staff's occupancy of buildings and too much to surface cleanings, in terms of both the practical and pedagogical impact.

I found fewer examples of libraries using their outdoor spaces to address "third space" needs. This role, while celebrated, can also be underappreciated for its equity impact. Precarious, substandard, and overcrowded housing is far too common in our society. A place to sit, read, be online, socialize, take some respite, and recharge one's batteries is essential to our well-being. For many, the library is the best or only available place for these soothing activities.

For many businesses in the pandemic—restaurants especially—outdoor pop-up spaces have been a lifeline. That the similar creation of library destination spaces in parking lots, patios, and street fronts has not been more common is something of a surprise.

The Denver Public Library (DPL) created outdoor library spaces at many of its branch locations in order to safely gather and provide essential services while the indoors are safely closed. These outdoor spaces operate alongside curbside pickup services, which are offered at all locations. The DPL's outdoor "technology access service" was launched, at first without publicity, at the Central Library on July 14, 2020. This popular and successful program was led and designed by the DPL's digital inclusion team as part of the library's Return to Buildings plan. By August, using outdoor spaces at 12 of its 26 locations, the library was providing laptops, free printing, tables, seating, shade canopies, and staff assistance. Laptops are cleaned between uses, and a library card is not required. Site selection was driven by digital equity needs, and the sites were furnished with existing tables and chairs.

The Denver Public Library also paired laptop lending with its bookmobile service, bringing essential technology access to outdoor spaces at shelters, resettlement facilities, and other emergency housing. The libraries' own facilities were purposefully developed with outdoor seating, which was never shuttered, and public Wi-Fi has been kept available at all locations continuously, 24/7. This provides low-risk, rudimentary digital access citywide, though one's own digital device is required.

The Denver city librarian, Michelle Jeske, tells me that they've had inquiries from many libraries about their outdoor model, and she remains surprised that this approach has not been more common. "Our thinking was, because this science is clear about outdoors being safer than indoors, when you *can* be outdoors. . . . Why not?" When the city had an early snow, they shuttered on

FIGURE 22.1 | The San Diego Public Library used patios at its Central Library and some branches for outdoor service, with on-site laptop computer lending. Photo by the author.

those days. "Which isn't hard. We sent out an e-mail to staff saying, 'not going to do this today.'" This practical spirit was behind their eventual reliance on the scientific community's guidance rather than that of the federal government.

HEROES

At this writing the United States is seeing COVID-19 cases peak again, but not evenly. Some regions have reached low prevalence, while in others the virus is widespread. Most states continue to face localized and rolling flare-ups, for how long we can only guess. As the epidemiologist Michael Osterholm put it in April, "I think people haven't understood that this isn't about the next couple of weeks. This is about the next two years."[3]

Our understanding of the transmission of the COVID-19 virus will continue to advance and new techniques of diagnosis, mitigation, surveillance, and treatment will emerge. In this environment, the ordinary lags between scientific knowledge and institutional guidance will remain consequential. And if the past six months are an indication, mixed messages will continue to buffet our response.

There's an understandable temptation, then, to wait for official adoption of the current scientific guidance. This, in turn, inspires a similarly understandable temptation to either go fully remote or to throw every cleaning supply and Plexiglas barrier at business as usual. But neither one of these approaches communicates what is and isn't high-risk. Neither one empowers our communities with low-risk practices they can take elsewhere. And neither approach creates sufficient alternatives to unsustainable social abstinence. Many, many libraries have instead shown a justified impatience. They've responded to the real risks, to the need for safe activities, and to the value of a simple, clear message. They're leading the way out of doors.

NOTES

1. The dominant institutional strategy of libraries over the past ten years has perhaps been "libraries equal education." Usually, this means that we announce libraries' value in terms of our contribution to learning, which in turn informs our priorities. I'm not sure we've given this strategy the debate it deserves, but that's another topic. In any case, one aspect of "libraries as educators" is a given: that through the example of our everyday practice and the rituals of library use, we communicate, and to a degree inculcate, what we value and what we know. We value reading to kids, and it can look like *this*. Social infrastructure is important. The destitute are full members of our

community. And so on. We can be more or less thoughtful about what our practice teaches and how we shape that together with our communities, but we're engaged in it as a matter of course.

2. Alexandra Lange, "How to Make the Most of COVID Winter," *Bloomberg CityLab*, September 11, 2020, www.bloomberg.com/news/articles/2020-09-11/how-to-prepare -for-a-coronavirus-winter. This article is an appeal to not abandon the wintry outdoors during the pandemic, with ideas that libraries can consider like windbreaks, patio heaters, straw bale seating, hot food trucks, s'more kits, hot chocolate carts, and more. Libraries' contributions can help ensure that these facilities are inclusive and equitable.

3. Quoted in Ed Yong, "Our Pandemic Summer," *The Atlantic*, April 14, 2020, www.theatlantic.com/health/archive/2020/04/pandemic-summer-coronavirus -reopening-back-normal/609940/.

APPENDIX

Understanding Your Library's Impact: Assessment and Evaluation of Virtual Services

— Emily Plagman —

The assessment and evaluation of virtual services help libraries understand patron impact, communicate their value to decision-makers, and understand opportunities to make improvements. Having a plan to assess your programs when you administer them will help ensure that you align your work with your library's goals, so that you can measure success. To this end, the Public Library Association (PLA) has developed resources to help libraries capture and understand their programs' impact. The PLA's Project Outcome (www.projectoutcome.org) is a *free* online toolkit designed to help public libraries understand and share the impact of essential library programs and services by providing simple surveys and an easy-to-use process for measuring and analyzing outcomes. Participating libraries are also provided with the resources and training support needed to apply their results and confidently advocate for their library's future. Project Outcome allows for the virtual measurement of programs across eight different topics, stores the results in a centralized location, and offers interactive data visualizations of the results. Here are some specific resources designed to support virtual activities and services.

MEASURING VIRTUAL PROGRAMS

www.projectoutcome.org/surveys-resources/measuring-virtual-programs
Online and remote programs and services raise new challenges for planning and evaluation. This resource outlines general strategies for survey distribution that can help increase response rates, including distribution methods and ways to frame communications to patrons. It also provides examples of how those methods can be applied to a few types of online and remote programs

and services that libraries offer, including virtual storytimes, grab-and-go kits, summer reading, and online programming for adults.

SAMPLE SURVEY CHECKLIST

www.projectoutcome.org/modyules/107
This guideline provides a short checklist based on common best practices that are used when designing a survey from scratch. It asks questions like, "Have you avoided jargon?" and "Could the wording be simplified?" The checklist is intended to help the reader think through the possible pitfalls when developing a survey, and it is also useful when drafting questions for any kind of in-person or virtual survey.

ALTERNATIVE DATA COLLECTION METHODS

www.projectoutcome.org/modyules/127
Using a measurement technique other than surveys to capture outcomes may be a better choice in certain instances. For example, library workers may want to receive in-depth feedback from patrons about the library space. In this and many other cases, library staff will have determined that a single survey will not provide enough information about the outcomes which need to be measured, and another method will be necessary. This resource provides summary information about other common measurement alternatives.

MAXIMIZING AND MEASURING VIRTUAL PROGRAMMING

www.ala.org/pla/education/onlinelearning/webinars/ondemand/maximizing
Developed in response to COVID-19, this on-demand webinar is designed to help libraries identify targeted outcomes to use when designing online programs, in order to maximize learning opportunities and measure the programs' resulting value for attendees. It helps library workers identify programming outcomes that are specifically geared to maximizing the online learning of participants; gain confidence in their ability to craft their own outcomes in order to measure the impact of online learning; draft at least one outcome for a planned online program; and understand how the Project Outcome system can be used to measure online programs and services.

--- -- -- -- -- -- -- -- -- -- -- -- -- --

Project Outcome was designed to help public libraries understand and share the true impact of their services and programs—arming libraries with the data they need to continue that impact. You can use the toolkit's simple survey instruments to demonstrate the value of your virtual library programs and services, make plans for improvement, and facilitate your decision-making as you plan future offerings.

ABOUT THE CONTRIBUTORS

VIRGINIA VASSAR AGGREY is the program manager for the Denver Public Library's Plaza program, which aims at connecting immigrants and refugees with the resources they need to thrive.

CHRISTOPHE ANDERSEN is the outreach and senior services librarian at the Northbrook Public Library in Illinois. Prior to his current position, he was the acquisitions and collection management librarian at Columbia College in Chicago, and was a member of the Technical Services Committee with the Consortium of Academic and Research Libraries in Illinois.

CORDELIA ANDERSON is the author of *Library Marketing and Communications: Strategies to Increase Relevance and Results.* During her decade at the Charlotte Mecklenburg Library in North Carolina, her team earned the inaugural *Library Journal* Marketer of the Year Award and two John Cotton Dana Awards. She now runs her own consulting company (www.cordeliaandersonpr.com).

DEEDEE BALDWIN is an assistant professor, history research librarian, and liaison to the Shackouls Honors College at the Mississippi State University Libraries. In 2019 she served as president of the Society of Mississippi Archivists.

CARRIE BANKS is the supervising librarian of the Brooklyn Public Library's Inclusive Services and the 2020 president of ASGCLA (a division of the American Library Association). She is the author of the revised edition of *Including Families of Children with Special Needs: A How-to-Do-It Manual for Librarians* and the coauthor (with Cindy Mediavilla) of *Libraries and Gardens: Growing Together.*

BECCA BOLAND is the supervisor of advisory services at the Skokie Public Library in Illinois. She is passionate about finding the best book for every reader and loves sharing her passion with fellow librarians (or anyone who will listen). She is the author of *Making the Most of Teen Library Volunteers: Energizing and Engaging Community*.

STESHA BRANDON is a longtime advocate for the literary arts. As the program director at Town Hall Seattle (https://townhallseattle.org/), and previously at the University Book Store, she specialized in developing compelling programs focused on arts and ideas. She is currently the literature and humanities program manager at the Seattle Public Library.

TIFFANY BREYNE is the communications coordinator at the Skokie Public Library in Illinois.

SHAUN BRILEY is the director of the Coronado Public Library in California. In 2016 he was named a *Library Journal* Mover & Shaker. He has initiated several innovative programs, including a community biology lab in a library, a crowd-sourced DNA bar-coding project, and a book club that provides pre-publication feedback to publishers.

JEFFREY T. DAVIS is a branch manager at the San Diego Public Library. He has worked in branch and central libraries from the South Bronx to downtown San Diego and in collection development and online services. He is the author of *The Collection All Around: Sharing Our Cities, Towns, and Natural Places*. His library design shingle is at libraryfresh.com.

NICANOR DIAZ is the Denver Public Library's immigrant services manager and the head of the Cultural Inclusivity Department. He has been working in libraries with underserved populations for over fifteen years.

STEPHANIE FRUHLING is an information services librarian at the Des Moines Public Library.

KATE HALL is the executive director of the Northbrook Public Library in Illinois. She is active in library consortia, the Reaching Across Illinois Library System, and the Illinois Library Association. She is a past chair of the Director's University, an intensive training program for new Illinois public library directors, and is the coauthor of *The Public Library Director's Toolkit*.

SUZANNE DeKEYZER JAMES is the public relations officer at the Bienville Parish Public Library in Louisiana.

ALLAN M. KLEIMAN is the director of the Montville Township Public Library in New Jersey, and is the current chair of RUSA's RSS Library Service to an Aging Population Committee.

BARBARA KLIPPER is a retired youth services librarian and the author of *Programming for Children and Teens with Autism Spectrum Disorder*. She started the Special Needs Center at the Ferguson Library in Stamford, Connecticut, and founded the Autism Welcome Here: Library Programs, Services and More grant.

PAIGE KNOTTS is a senior librarian at the Des Moines Public Library.

SARAH LANE is an information services librarian at the Des Moines Public Library.

CHERYL A. LANG is the manager of the Midwest Genealogy Center, a part of the Mid-Continent Public Library system in Independence, Missouri. She currently serves on the board of the Missouri State Genealogical Association and belongs to several local genealogy societies. There is nothing that she enjoys more than helping folks find their family history.

CINDY MEDIAVILLA is a freelance library consultant who evaluates grant programs and teaches workshops on a variety of topics. She has written or coauthored several books for the ALA, including *Libraries and Gardens: Growing Together* and *Creating & Managing the Full-Service Homework Center*. Cindy's MLS and PhD degrees are both from UCLA.

BOBBI L. NEWMAN is the community engagement and outreach specialist at the Network of the National Library of Medicine, Greater Midwest Region, at the University of Iowa. She blogs at https://librarianbyday.net and is the coauthor of the forthcoming book *Fostering Wellness in the Library Workplace*.

RACHEL PAYNE is the coordinator of early childhood services at the Brooklyn Public Library.

FATIMA PERKINS is the current vice chair/chair elect of RUSA's Reference Services Section and the director of community outreach and advocacy at the Western Reserve Area Agency on Aging in Ohio. As a social gerontologist and librarian, she has developed and implemented programs that educate, engage, and empower mature audiences.

EMILY PLAGMAN is the Manager, QI and Evaluation at American Academy of Pediatrics. Prior to that she served as project manager for PLA's performance measurement initiative, Project Outcome. She earned her master's degree in international public affairs at the University of Wisconsin.

JESSICA RALLI is the coordinator of early literacy programs at the Brooklyn Public Library.

GILLIAN ROBBINS is a library supervisor in the Business Resource and Innovation Center (BRIC) at the Free Library of Philadelphia. She specializes in curating information, providing research services, and coordinating programming and special events for entrepreneurs. She was instrumental in developing a new service model for the BRIC.

LAUREN SEEGMILLER is librarian, reference services, at the Denver Public Library.

CAITLIN SEIFRITZ has worked for the Free Library of Philadelphia for eight years in various roles. She is currently a library supervisor in the Free Library's Business Resource and Innovation Center, and specializes in services for nonprofit organizations. Before becoming a librarian, Caitlin worked for a small, Brooklyn-based nonprofit. She received her MLS from the Pratt Institute.

NAGHEM SWADE coordinates all cultural inclusivity programming for the Denver Public Library.

LUKE THOMPSON is a tech associate at the Evanston Public Library in Illinois. He holds a PhD in East Asian languages and cultures from Columbia University, and taught courses on religious studies and Buddhist studies at colleges and prisons in New York and Illinois prior to entering the world of library tech services.

ASHLEY WELKE is the regional coordinator at the Pioneer Library System in central Oklahoma.

SUZANNE WULF is the head of digital services at the Niles-Maine District Library in Illinois. She spearheads innovative initiatives and is dedicated to providing equitable access to technology. She oversees a busy technology center, makerspace, and media lab. Additionally, she developed a circulating technology collection and introduced virtual reality experiences to the community.

INDEX

Index